SAN MIGUEL
DE ALLENDE, MEXICO

Acclaim for Rick Skwiot

Christmas at Long Lake: A Childhood Memory

"Skwiot's vivid descriptions of the physical and emotional landscape...are poignant, entertaining, and instructional...There is magic in this depiction of a setting and a way of life that can be described only as Edenic."
— *Library Journal*

"Rick Skwiot works his own magic...As usual, Skwiot's writing is sure...And his tale has a gritty, blue-collar cachet...This is good reading."
— *Kansas City Star*

"Skwiot's memories of the grandmothers are rich and poignant, and the descriptive detail shimmers."
— *St. Louis Post-Dispatch*

"...an elegant evocation not only of a particular time and place but also of the way childhood memories set up a permanent residence in our hearts. This is a lovely, elegiac book."
— Robert Olen Butler, Pulitzer Prize-winning author of
   A Good Scent from a Strange Mountain

Sleeping with Pancho Villa

"A thoughtfully layered backdrop of Mexican culture... impressively crafted labyrinthine setting...Snappy and often funny dialogue."
— *Publishers Weekly*

"Life in a Mexican town...laid out beautifully...A skillfully written portrait of an entire community. Highly recommended."
— *Library Journal*

"This book alone heralds the arrival of a great new writer."
— *The Colorado Springs Independent*

SAN MIGUEL
DE ALLENDE, MEXICO

MEMOIR OF A SENSUAL QUEST FOR SPIRITUAL HEALING

BY

RICK SKWIOT

ANTAEUS BOOKS

San Miguel de Allende, Mexico:
Memoir of a Sensual Quest for Spiritual Healing

ISBN 978-0-9828591-0-0
Library of Congress Control Number: 2010910336

Book design by Amy McAdams
www.amymcadams.com

www.san-miguel-de-allende-mexico.net

To
Jayne Navarre

Contents

Preface

When friends read my fiction they often suggest that I am merely writing autobiography, and when they read my autobiographical writing they accuse me of just making it all up. While that may say less about my approach as novelist or memoirist than about their human nature, it does suggest to me that my life as I present it claims certain fantastical or miraculous elements that are hard to believe.

That seemingly holds true as well in this work, which chronicles my early years in Mexico, where I went looking for a miracle and, finding many, happily jettisoned much rational gringo cargo that had long burdened me. As I now revisit the scenes depicted here it's hard for me to believe that many actually occurred, for they seem so surreal. But even Salvador Dali had to admit after he first visited Mexico, "It's the most surreal place I've seen."

All that aside, what matters here in the following memoir is that I am not just making it all up. This book presents a factual recounting, albeit from my own highly personal perspective, drawn in large part from extensive journals that I kept during my Mexican sojourns. Thus, though nominally a memoir this work is in large part on-the-scene reporting distilled through a certain retrospective insight gained from two decades' distance.

However, I have changed some names or blurred certain identities out of delicacy and a desire not to injure or expose friends who were trusting, loyal and charitable, and whose friendship I still cherish across the years and the miles.

SAN MIGUEL
DE ALLENDE, MEXICO

PART ONE

I

Ni Modo

My left ankle bent awkwardly beneath me as I came down with a rebound on the fissured concrete court by the *chorro*. As I lay there moaning, players gathered round shaking their heads and shrugging, as if examining a dead burro. One, eager to continue the game, said, "Ni modo," a vague, untranslatable Mexican phrase indicating helplessness and/ or indifference.

With a teammate's aid I managed to hobble back to my *casita* facing the park. The ankle swelled, turned purple, and throbbed. I figured I had broken it but felt a resignation that I would not have thought myself capable of just months earlier. The previous summer in St. Louis when I'd fractured my hand playing basketball, it struck me as a tragedy. Six weeks without hoops, swimming, or biking. I couldn't even type properly, which made my freelance writing work even more tedious and time-consuming. I didn't know what to do with myself. For the good part of two months I was angry over it and cursed my bad luck. But now I found myself thinking that this current misfortune had occurred for a reason. Maybe with my leg in a cast I'd read more and encounter a book that would change my life. Or perhaps I'd begin writing my masterpiece. Or maybe I'd meet a beautiful doctor. Who knew? It was out of my hands, so why fight it? Ni modo.

What had happened to me in San Miguel de Allende? Something, certainly. I hardly recognized myself. I recalled my first bus trip to San Miguel but months earlier and remembered saying a prayer of sorts as the bus cut the arid countryside. I'd prayed for deliverance, that I might somehow be touched by whatever Mexico would bring me and changed by it. That I might somehow cure myself of the inner deadness that had settled on me like an obliterating fog, in which I had lost myself. And now, in a way I could have never predicted, my prayer had been answered, at least in part. I smiled at my recollection of a hand-lettered sign the driver of that first bus had affixed above the rearview mirror. It read: "No deje su basura en el autobús. Tírela por la ventana."—Do not leave your trash on the bus. Throw it out the window.

At the time I couldn't appreciate such selfish thinking. But now, after knowing Licha, Ernesto, Martina, Ramos, and other Mexicans who lived their lives not with Puritan guilt and restraint but with audacity, verve, and a crude élan born of Conquistador and Aztec blood, I'd come to appreciate the value of such a philosophy. In fact it seemed a worthy mantra for me, a reminder to discard all my psychic trash—the self-doubts, shame, and regrets—so it wouldn't clutter my consciousness and impede my progress. From now on, I vowed, I'd be moving down the road on a clean bus. Though I would find it a difficult oath to keep.

Later that evening Licha came by to lure me out for a drink. She gasped when she saw my injury and said: "Why did you do this to me?"

I thought I had misheard her, had somehow garbled her rapid, Mexico City Spanish.

"¿Mande?"

She reiterated: "¿Por qué, por qué, por qué? Now who will I dance with?"

I pursed my lips and studied her from the cushioned banquette where I lay before a cold fireplace. She was an elegant creature, tall and svelte. She stood hands on hips, nostrils flaring, black eyes cold. I said: "Lo siento, Licha. Forgive me. I hadn't thought how this might inconvenience you. I was thinking only of myself and of how fucking much my ankle hurt."

She got herself a Coke from the refrigerator and stood over me tapping her toe on the stone floor. "It looks bad. You need an x-ray. I will come tomorrow to take you."

"Gracias. I need some help."

After fetching me a beer from the fridge, she prepared to leave, presumably to find a new dance partner. She paused at the door, turned back to me biting her lip, and said: "Ay, Rick, why did you do this to me?"

I didn't understand its significance yet, but she did. She saw where it would lead.

*

She showed up the next morning as promised and called a taxi on the phone in the main house. We rode to a small clinic near the *jardín*, Nuestra Señora de la Salud, which, Licha claimed, housed the only x-ray machine this side of Celaya. As I struggled to pry myself from the back seat she put her hand to her mouth and began to laugh.

"What's so damn funny?" I barked in English.

She lifted her chin toward the alley abutting the clinic. "Mira."

There the arse end of a thoroughbred protruded through opened French doors. Its owner, a local *patrón*, had brought it in to have its front leg x-rayed, I soon learned, when it came up lame. I shook my head. Licha said: "Solamente en México."

Inside, a stoic, gray-haired *campesino* with a broken arm sat patiently awaiting his turn while they x-rayed the horse. I could see the bone pressing against his skin. When the radiologist came out and saw me, a gringo, a paying customer, he wanted to take me first, but I told him I could wait till he x-rayed the old man. Soon, however, with x-rays in hand we rode to the government clinic on the other side of town. Licha helped me inside then took the taxi on to the hotel where she worked.

In a dusty examination room I waited to see Dr. Ramos, who'd been recommended to me as an American-trained physician who spoke English. My Spanish was improving. I was using the future, subjunctive, and past-perfect tenses, and even dreaming in it. But the previous night I had to look up the words for tendon, ligament, and ankle, and so decided to call on Ramos.

I had seen him about town driving a camouflaged Volkswagen jeep fitted, for some reason, with dozens of seemingly useless antennas. And I had heard stories of Ramos, The Flying Doctor, who was known for neglecting to gas up his Cessna and making forced landings all over the state. I can't recall why this might have inspired confidence in his medical skills.

Soon, wearing a mis-buttoned and wrinkled white lab coat, a bearded Ramos sauntered into the examining room hands-in-pockets. By way of introduction he strode to me and flicked the pack of Faros in my shirt pocket with the back of his hand. "What are those, gringo?" he asked in accented English.

"Well, cigarettes."

He held out his hand. "Give them to me."

I did as he said.

"Smoking is bad for the health," he said shaking the pack at me. Then he took one out, lit it up, and placed the remainder in his pocket.

I handed him the brown envelope containing my x-rays. He held them up, walking to the window. "Here and here: two fissures. You have broken your ankle. How did you manage that?"

"Playing basketball."

"In the league?"

I nodded then shook my head. "For the first time in my life I got to play the pivot. Now this."

For once I was the tallest man on the team. Up north I had always been a guard with a spotty outside shot, an offensive liability. In Mexico, however, I was the Big White Banger, the man positioned in the paint, though there was little paint left on the concrete court. I played a graceful, balletic game, I felt, hitting sky-hooks, controlling the boards, and feeding the wingman on fast breaks. In Mexico I was a relative star.

Ramos made a pitching motion. "I play baseball on Sundays. La Liga de la última oportunidad, the Last Chance League. I still have my curve. But the fastball…" He waved good-bye to it with my x-rays. He turned to examine the swollen limb. "The worst is the soft-tissue damage. You'll need a cast. But it's too bloated now. Keep it elevated and come back in a week."

A week! I had hoped to have a walking cast slapped on and to be hobbling around town that night. I tried to be philosophical: So be it; I'll get some reading in, I told myself, but with little enthusiasm.

As I was leaving the clinic, hopping precariously on one foot, they wheeled in an elderly British woman who had been trampled by a runaway burro. She lay on a gurney, bruised and bleeding, her hip apparently broken. Ramos approached and stood over her, shaking his head and dusting her with ashes from the cigarette in his lips. He waved an admonishing finger at her and asked, "And now what have we been doing?"

*

It seemed the longest week of my life, spent in substantial isolation. Here, unlike the apartment at Lupe's that I would later occupy, there was no garden in which to sit and read, no amiable *dueña* eager to talk philosophy. I had ample floor space—not an amenity when barely ambulatory—including a sun-lit studio up narrow stairs that I now could not easily negotiate. Further, downstairs, where I was forced to remain, little light came through a lone, north-facing window on the shady park. Dank and cheerless, the room resembled more a cave than civilized human habitation, and, as I was soon to learn, I had just begun my hibernation.

Having no phone or television had not been a great handicap previously. Few of my friends there had phones; when I needed to talk to someone, I'd go find him. And a TV was next to worthless then, in the pre-cable-TV days of 1983. The hotel where I first stayed had a television in the lobby that got a snowy picture from one distant station. Now, however, being confined to my cave with a stack of books and a clock radio that played only Mexican pop tunes made me wish for other diversions. By Sunday I was so booked-out and bored that I listened to a *pase-por-pase* account of a bullfight from Mexico City. Evenings, through my window, I heard school children in the street rehearsing songs for an upcoming Christmas pageant. Their sweet voices reminded me that outside my cell life went on without me.

Fortunately the maid for the main house, Taide, was accommodating. She arranged to borrow some homemade crutches that helped me move about my home. She brought me boiled water for drinking. From the *casa grande* she made telephone calls for me and even went to the market each day and cooked my afternoon meal. But afterward she left for her home on the other side of town, and I was left to myself.

I was particularly grateful for Taide's aid since Licha had all but disappeared. She came by once at siesta. We soon moved to the brass bed on the elevated sleeping alcove that faced the kitchen and living room. But being of a lively nature she kept kicking my ankle, making me yelp in pain. Then, just as she became somewhat accommodated to my injury, Taide walked in. The maid moved to the kitchen and began washing dishes. I reached for the sheet and called across the room:

"¿Taide…?"

"¿Sí?"

"Taide…"

She turned and gazed at me. Then she noticed Licha shaking in glee beneath the sheet.

"Ah. Perdón." She dried her hands on a towel and went back out the front door.

I sat leaning back on my elbows. I had waited days for some company. I had dreamed of Licha. Now this. I turned to look at her. When she saw my sullen expression she exploded in laughter.

"I don't find it particularly amusing."

"But why did you stop, Rick? I was just starting to enjoy myself." She laughed even harder.

I let my eyes lay on her a moment then reached for a cigarette. "Yeah, me too. But that damn maid broke my concentration."

She leaned over and laid her arm across my shoulders. "Ay, Rick. You try to speak our language and live like us. But you will never be a true mejicano if you can't make love with people watching."

*

I can't quite recall how I met Licha. Perhaps Jesús, the night manager at the hotel where I first stayed, introduced us in a bar. At the time, San Miguel de Allende was a small town with a small number of venues to drink and dance. Licha and I, both at loose ends, would likely have found each other sooner or later.

When she first asked me to dance I resisted, saying I didn't know how to salsa, concerned about how I might look. She pulled me to the dance floor in the dark, candle-lit room. Above us a band—flute, acoustic guitar, old double bass, African drums—poured out a flowing Caribbean sound that was part sea and part jungle, smooth yet primitive. She wore black, adding to her dark mystery. Dark irises, black eyelashes feathering high cheekbones, black hair falling across her forehead. Her lips pouty, her hips moving rhythmically inside the black dress like dark waves, her skin creamy cocoa. A fortunate mix of Aztec, Moor, and Spaniard, of conqueror and conquered. Soon, focused on her and not myself, I began to move with her.

I recall us getting *bien borrachos* on tequila that night and ending up in my hotel room for a drunken frolic. But it quickly became more than that. Since Licha could not cook and at first I had no kitchen, we frequently ate out together for each other's company. She helped me with my Spanish, I corrected her English. We shared an interest in books, a liking for rough humor, and an arrogance that kept our conversations lively. We laughed a lot, for there seemed much to be amused by in Mexico, particularly if one had an eye for irony and a taste for tragicomedy. But Licha saw that I had come for more than just laughs.

One night in a dark cellar lounge where a young Mexican folksinger strummed a guitar, she looked across the table and said, "You have come here for a reason."

"Which is?"

"To change your life."

I felt myself redden. To deter any delving into my inner struggle, I said: "It has changed already. If I had stayed home, I would be missing out on so much."

Licha blew out a stream of cigarette smoke. "Like me."

"Sí, a great deprivation. Before meeting you my life was not half so interesting."

"De veras. But we live now. I do not care what you did before I knew you or what you do when you are not with me."

"Are you sure?"

"Only now matters. I want to live fast, to burn quickly and brightly like straw, and die young."

"Esta filosofía es muy mejicana y muy romántica."

"Sí, I am very Mexican and live in the present. I do not believe in reincarnation or plastic surgery like your gringas. But since I am Mexican, I will be totally and faithfully yours no matter what you do until you get on the bus to leave."

We were joined by an American couple who knew Licha from the hotel. They soon began talking about a business they were starting, flying expatriate Americans back to the

States for acute medical care when needed, thus avoiding Mexican doctors and hospitals. Licha stood, bid me good-night, and headed for the door. By the time I paid the bill and followed her outside, she was gone.

Next day when I mentioned the incident, she apologized. "I am sorry, Rick, but I was thinking that I might die in my sleep and didn't want to spend my last hours with sonofabitches."

II
Only in Mexico

As I took stock during my solitude, waiting for my swollen ankle to shrink, I saw that Mexico and Mexicans had infected me in a way I could not have imagined. Licha had become a conduit through which I came to know scores of *sanmiguelenses* and transplants from both hemispheres. Mexico drew gringos who were searching or hiding, who had come to be healed or reinvented—or, in my case, both. San Miguel de Allende lured Mexican and other Latin American men and women for similar reasons. Both Anglophones and Latinos were pivotal in my reawakening, but the Mexicans offered me something unique.

To my rational gringo perceptions they seemed unusually warm, open, human, and happily fallible to an eccentric extent. They did not hide their failings, peccadilloes, lusts, and hatreds as brooding northerners did. Rather, they aired them, reveled in them, and fed them. Instead of cluttering their psyches with the debris of envy, hypocrisy, or regret, they exposed their sins and shortcomings, often with humor and a lack of self-consciousness or contrition that astounded me. After having spent a lifetime hiding who I was and fabricating a persona I wasn't, their self-love and self-acceptance came as a liberating revelation. For most Mexicans I met, well-being meant following your heart and not the herd. Somehow the Catholicism, the Indian blood, and the tragic land, Mexico, *La Chingadera*, the Fucked One, made them philosophic and original in ways few gringos could aspire to.

I recall the Mexico City cabbie who raced through the dark night despite my protestations: "I am in no hurry. More slowly, por favor." But he kept on flying down narrow streets toward my hotel, passing other vehicles, terrifying pedestrians, and running traffic lights. Finally, unnerved, I scolded him: "Don't you know that red means stop?"

As we zoomed through another red light he gestured toward it in passing and explained: "It is only a suggestion."

The sanmiguelense Ernesto was also philosophic. Once, when he took me to a vaudeville show passing through town that fall, he sat atypically silent, watching a full-figured dancer bump and grind to a three-piece orchestra. When the music stopped, he applauded thoughtfully and leaned to me.

"Tell me, Rick. Did you ever know an intelligent woman with big breasts?" He sighed. "Ah, nature is funny."

But he was philosophic about more than women. Arrested once for running wetbacks across the Rio Grande, he spent a month in a Texas jail. But for Ernesto it was not time wasted. While incarcerated he and nine other *coyotes* there formed an organization that sent ten thousand illegals across the border in the next two months.

"There's only one thing worth doing in this world," he told me, "and that's helping other people." His words struck me, for it was the same conclusion drawn by Tolstoy, whom I was then reading.

But like most people, Ernesto had trouble living up to an abstract, altruistic philosophy, in part because of his love for the jug. "I'm just a goddamned alcoholic," he often told me, and confirmed it on numerous occasions.

Once, we sat down together at a low table in La Fragua, but the waiters ignored us. When Efrín, who played point guard on my park-league basketball team, passed with his tray I grabbed him.

"¿Qué pasa, amigo? Why can't we get a drink?"

"Lo siento, but I am not permitted."

"¿Por qué?"

"Because of what happened Saturday night."

Ernesto and I looked at each other and shrugged.

"What happened Saturday?"

Efrín glanced over his shoulder. "The fight where your

friend"—here he nodded at Ernesto—"bit the ear of the patrón Rafael."

I looked at Ernesto, who spread his palms and raised his eyebrows. "It's possible."

But like other Mexicans and Mexico itself, Ernesto could break your heart with his woes. On the night before I left San Miguel the first time, he brought me a cane from his shop to help me move about on my cast. For once he was sober, and somber. The previous day he had missed the annual father-son soccer match because he was too hung-over to play.

"I'm just a goddamned alcoholic," he reiterated.

Ernesto's Spanish *compadre* Arquimedes was a philosopher as well. Despite his long years in Mexico he spoke Spanish with an exacting, hard-edged lisp that distinguished his tongue from the musical dialect of the local Mexicans. Once, as we sat in the town square chatting about Mexico's corrupt politics, its Third World economics, and its ongoing social degeneration, a horribly deformed campesino edged past us over the smooth stones. His head lay to the side as if his neck were too weak to support it, a distant look of long-suffering in his eyes. Both hands clutched at his chest, fingers knotted and seemingly paralyzed. He dragged a near-useless left leg behind him, moving through the jardín one step at a time.

Arquimedes and I both fell mute, humbled by this poor creature's ongoing struggle while we sat in the shade and bitched about life. Our heads turned in unison as we watched him shuffle to the low end of the square and move down the stone steps one by one. When he was gone, Arquimedes still stared after him and said:

"Compared to the United States or Spain, Mexico may be a fucked-up place. But at least here a man can walk in whatever way he chooses." Then he laughed so hard that tears came to his eyes.

*

If Mexican men were philosophic and tough-minded, Mexican women seemed ethereal and enveloping, like comforting down. Most exuded a warmth, gaiety, and spirituality that differentiated them not only from their male compatriots but also from more masculine and materialistic North American women.

One of the first I met was an artist, Ilena, who taught on occasion at the Instituto Allende on the lower side of town. She had lived for a time with the *indígenas* in the jungles of Chiapas and invoked Tlaloc, Quetzalcoatl, and other ancient gods. She claimed to heal with herbs and magic, about which I was dubious. Once she cured my hiccups by taking a red thread from the hem of her skirt, wetting it on her tongue, and curling it on my forehead. Still I was unimpressed.

At the home of her friend Silvia I later witnessed a more convincing display. As we entered, we heard Silvia's young daughter crying upstairs. She had been doing so all day, Silvia said, and running a fever.

I followed Ilena to the little girl's bedroom. After examining the child, Ilena went downstairs and returned with a fist of dried basil stalks and a raw egg. She placed the herbs under the child's pillow, passed the egg over her body as she chanted incomprehensible Indian phrases, then broke the egg into a glass of cold water, which she placed on the nightstand.

We went back downstairs and returned to the child's bedside an hour later. The little girl was sleeping quietly, her forehead was cool, and the egg had cooked solid.

*

To me Licha embodied Mexico, or at least an eccentric part of it. That season she and I frequently went to La Fragua, Mamma Mia's, and Laberintos to drink and dance, usually with her best friend, Martina, who had recently moved there from Mexico City with Licha. Martina was always quietly looking for a man and occasionally found one to take home. But usually she preferred the company of Licha and me, preferred to take nothing seriously. Though it was hard to take things too seriously when Licha was around.

One evening, since she was trying to lose three kilos, Licha and I had decided to eat a light supper in. She wanted to help prepare it, but her aid was limited. Although she was thirty-three and had been married for seven years, she had never prepared a meal, having had maids and cooks when growing up and before divorcing. After that, when still living in Mexico City, she ate out every night with her son. She had wanted to find a lover who could cook but never had any luck locating him.

Despite her kitchen inexperience she told me she could fix salad. So I told her to wash the lettuce. She looked at the head of leaf lettuce, pursing her lips. I went to fetch a bottle of wine from the cupboard. When I returned she was filling the sink with hot, soapy water. I stopped her before she plunged the lettuce into it, and showed her how to wash the leaves in cold water and dry them with a towel.

As I began chopping onion and pepper for an omelet, she asked: "What can I do now?"

I gave her a cucumber and carrot, along with a vegetable peeler. "Peel and slice these for the salad."

She held the vegetable peeler up before her eyes, turning it back and forth like an archeologist who has just unearthed some strange artifact. Then, satisfied that she had divined its function, she began beating the cucumber with it. This I found enchanting. To me she was like an exotic hothouse bloom: beautiful, pampered, solely ornamental. She reinforced this view by asking, as she chewed her omelet:

"¿Quién inventó la comida?"

I stared at her to see if she was serious. She repeated:

"Who invented food? Just think of all those poor people sitting around starving."

*

On one occasion Licha took the afternoon bus to Celaya to visit her gynecologist. She wanted him to replace her I.U.D., which had somehow gotten dislodged. When she returned that night she dropped by to take me out for a drink. But as we sat sipping at La Fragua I could tell that something bothered her and figured it had to do with her doctor visit.

"Estás preocupada. Díme, Licha. ¿Qué te molesta?"

She shook her head. "Nada. I am fine."

"What did the doctor tell you?"

She looked away.

I asked, "¿Estás embarazada?"—the peculiar Spanish word for pregnant.

She shook her head. "No. But he had to remove my device and cannot replace it for a week. So if you want to find another woman I understand."

"Maybe this is a sign from God: time for us to make a Mexican baby."

"Ay, my firecracker, you are drunk. Find someone else for that."

"No, gracias," I said. "I am happy going through the motions with you."

She laughed, but I could see she still needed reassuring and thought to buy her a small gift.

But by the next day, the Day of the Dead, I had forgotten my intention of shopping for a silver necklace. Instead I joined a throng of shuffling campesinos and sanmiguelenses moving down the dusty Ancha de San Antonio to the Panteón, where families came to share a meal with their dead kin. They decorated the crypts with flowers and photographs of the departed and, at the lush, shady, high end of the cemetery, sat upon the marble slabs covering the dead, munching tortillas and sipping Coca-Cola.

Over my years in Mexico I came to sense that to Mexicans death and life were merely different phases of an overarching existence, a view that assumed spirituality as a given. More than once when I asked Mexicans about their families I was told, "I have five children: two married daughters, a son in Morelia, and two babies in the cemetery," or some variation.

This blurring of life and death manifested itself in their art as well, particularly in the skeleton sugar sculptures, which vendors hawked outside the graveyard as I left. This delicate craft depicted sweet, diminutive sombrero-wearing skeletons riding skeleton horses, dancing to the music of skeleton mariachis, and marrying skeleton brides.

As I studied a wedding tableau with a bone priest uniting a deathly couple, a cognizance of the brevity of life—the blue skies, winging birds, and warm flesh—swept through me like a dark wind whistling through my rib cage. A graffito call-to-action came to mind, one I had seen scribbled on the wall above the urinal at La Fragua: "Tu esqueleto es vivo"—your skeleton is alive.

In the next stall another vendor sold egg-sized sugar

skulls on which he had etched in ink across the foreheads common names: Roberto, Susana, Guillermo, Christina, Marta, Luis…I studied them for a minute then asked:

"¿Hay una 'Licha'?"

He shook his head. "No, but I will make you one."

That evening as the sun set over the mountains, I walked from my casita past the chorro and up the hill to Licha's home on the Calle Hospicio, where I presented the personalized sugar skull to her. She cradled it in her palm, staring into its eye sockets and caressing its bony pate. Then she positioned it on the mantel between a photograph of her son and a crucifix.

*

Before I met Licha and was pulled outward to mix in the life of the town, I was turned inside looking for answers. At a hotel on the outskirts where I had first secluded myself, I was immersed in writing a play based on my recent marital breakup. I sat in a straight-backed chair as if in penance, clacking away on a borrowed typewriter and pouring out the roman à clef, oblivious to the mosquitoes swarming through the opened balcony door to the lamp beside me.

After I had written a few drafts I met a retired couple with some stage experience who agreed to do a reading of the play at my casita. Monty was a retired British army officer; his wife, Fernanda, a Hungarian refugee whom he had helped escape the Nazis. Despite their having forty years on the characters in the play, they gave a haunting candlelit reading that made Licha, Sid, Eduardo, Martina, Jesús, and me believe that the graying Fernanda was a dark-haired beauty of twenty-eight and Monty her impetuous young husband.

But after the reading, while the cast and audience shared bottles of wine, Licha fell silent and brooding. When I asked what bothered her she snorted at me and simply said: "¡Gringas!" Soon, claiming she had to get up early, she stomped out and up the hill to her home.

The next day when I chided her about her seeming jealousy and her previous claim to indifference about my prior behavior, she looked at me, shrugged, and said: "Ni modo. I was born that way." Then she turned from me and never again mentioned it.

III
De Efe

San Miguel de Allende was a haven for gringos like my-self but also, increasingly, for many Mexicans like Licha, who sought sanctuary from the growing urbanization and industrialization of Mexico. I came to better understand Licha and the allure San Miguel held for her ilk of amoral, self-loving Mexicans a month after we first met, when I traveled with her to Mexico City.

De Efe Mexicans call it, D.F., *El Distrito Federal*, or sim-ply México. Licha was a *chilanga*, a native of the capital, a choking city of twelve million then. I had agreed to accom-pany her there one weekend, hoping to get my tourist visa extended in the capital. (I should have known better. That Friday morning at the Gobernación, the department of the interior, I learned that the sole person in charge of tourist visas for the whole country had begun his weekend early.)

Licha had come to see her son, Alejandro, who lived with his lawyer father. That the father would get primary custody of a child in a Mexican divorce was not uncommon among her class. The daughter of an army general, she had married at nineteen into a wealthy family of lawyers and judges and into a life of suffocating ease and scrutiny. Servants did all the housework, cooking, and gardening. Licha was expected to travel by chauffeured car each morning to take coffee with her mother-in-law and sisters-in-law. Then she was free to do as she pleased: to shop, to visit her mother and married (but not unmarried) girlfriends, or to see a movie. But always escorted, purportedly for her safety in the teeming city, by the chauffeur, who'd sit two rows behind her in the movie theater. Licha spent a lot of time alone, reading. She suspected that her husband, like many men of his class, kept a mistress at a *casa chica* somewhere in De Efe.

I never doubted Licha's accounts of her married life, which she gave only reluctantly and with an anger in her eye that I would not have wanted focused on me. Further, she was so clueless about household chores that I figured she had to have had servants her whole life. Also, I had heard stories of marital malpractice from Mexican women of all classes. Women whose husbands would not let them smoke. Wives who, like Licha, were not allowed to travel un-chaperoned or attend classes. Women who were required to devote themselves to the maintenance of rigid traditions, fulfilling endless social obligations—christenings, *quinces*, birthday parties, saint's day celebrations, weddings, and funerals—with a dizzying number of in-laws. Nor was physical abuse uncommon. All this with macho husbands who often were having sex with other women or men.

As a result, many educated and independent young Mexican women like Licha, informed and emboldened by feminist movements in Europe and America, opted out of ossified Mexican marriage. But with few educated and non-traditional men about, some turned to lesbianism. Others sought out less tradition-bound European and American men.

That Thursday afternoon I had met Licha at the hotel when she got off work, and we walked down the hill to the dusty San Miguel bus-plaza. There we caught a grimy, smoke-spewing *Flecha Amarilla* headed for De Efe, some five hours distant, and settled back amid campesinos and workers on their way to San Juan del Río and Querétaro.

I tried to sleep, but the lowering sun came streaming through the window of the stuffy bus. Licha and I had been out dancing the night before, locals' night at the disco, when the usual cover charge was lifted. We'd met Martina at La Fragua at nine-thirty for drinks and near midnight walked down the hill to Laberintos. There we danced and drank until four, leaving then only because both women had to work in the morning. As a result I was, typical of Thursdays, tired and hung-over.

I tried to open the window, but the latch was missing, and I thought of The Man with the Steel Teeth. I'd heard his legend from a friend who claimed to have met him. An American CIA operative who had lost his real teeth in Vietnam, he traveled about Mexico ferreting out information on radical groups. But he had seemingly lost more than his teeth in Vietnam, for he always carried in his coat pocket a miniature tool kit of screwdriver, pliers, hammer, wire, screws, nails, nuts, and bolts. With it he tried to fix Mexico, which had been left in disrepair. He leveled beds in hotel rooms, tightened legs on restaurant tables, and reattached handles in taxis. If he had been in my bus seat he would have likely gerry-rigged a latch and opened the window that I could not.

It had been dark for hours when our bus pulled into the capital's Terminal del Norte. We bought a taxi voucher and queued for a cab. Then, since we were headed to the far south side of the city and taxis were scarce, we were shoved into a small cab with four other passengers, along with their plastic sacks and paper-wrapped packages.

We sat in the back seat, Licha pressed against the left door, me against the right. Between us sat two stoic mestizas clutching *bolsas* on their laps. The taxi moved silently through the cool night. I lay my head against the glass and finally dozed. But then a raucous yelp broke inside the packed cab. I woke with heart thumping, turned and saw the woman next to me tucking the head of a rooster back inside the plastic sack on her lap. Licha looked away, hand over her mouth, trying to stifle her laughter and turning dark red from the effort. A minute later when she had regained control, she got my attention and mouthed the words: "Only in Mexico."

After an hour in the cramped cab we arrived at the home of Licha's ex-sister-in-law Griselda, who lived in a new two-bedroom apartment with her husband Armando and their son Armando Junior. Though no doubt considered luxurious and commodious by the millions of Mexicans ringing the capital in shantytowns, the building seemed flimsy and a potential hazard in earthquake territory. And, like many Mexican structures, it stood uncompleted. The hallways were but partially painted and light bulbs there dangled from wires. I learned that Griselda and Armando had moved in three years earlier.

But more bothering was the smell. Somewhere in the darkened valley stood a paper mill that spread a putrid cloud across the sky day and night. I supposed one got used to it after three years.

However, once inside the apartment I forgot about it. Griselda was beautiful and charming and soon pulled me aside conspiratorially to share a flattering letter that Licha had written her about me. Armando, a mechanical engineer, brought out drawings of an invention he was working on, a wind-resistant bicycle. Armandito, just six, sat on my lap smiling and holding my hand. It was like coming home for the holidays but without all the family baggage.

Since I had not eaten since lunchtime and the women wanted to talk, Armando took me to a nearby restaurant in a new shopping mall. I guess he thought that as an American that's what I'd want. He ordered us beer and shots of tequila and began telling me of his recent business trip to Los Angeles.

Armando could not speak English. Yet, for the benefit of the middle-class Mexicans seated around us who perhaps had not noticed that he was in the company of a gringo, he did so anyway. At least on occasion he threw in a few English words, the most Anglo-Saxon he could muster.

What he found most amusing on his American trip he had encountered at a sex shop. With tears of mirth he related his discovery of inflatable American "party dolls."

"Primero, they inflar,..." Armando made a pumping motion. "Then...then they fook it! Ha ha ha ha! They fook it!"

Armando was nearly falling off his chair in delight over this bit of Americana. I glanced at two prim women seated next to us, but they seemed not to hear Armando or be offended by his four-letter words in this land of five-, six-, and seven-letter expletives.

While I ate, Armando drank, patting a premature paunch and stating he was on a diet. He talked more of his invention and laid out our plan for Saturday: Licha would visit her son. Armandito would go with his aunt for his piano lesson. Griselda would clean house, as was her custom on Saturdays. And Armando and I, under the guise of attending the horse races at the Hipódromo, would go to a brothel near the Plaza Garibaldi and get laid.

"Yes," he said winking. "We go fooking."

*

Next morning Licha went to visit her son, Alejandro, as planned. Armandito's aunt picked him up for his piano lesson. Armando and I walked downstairs to his car, ostensibly on our way to the Hipódromo, Griselda following.

I had no great desire to go fooking as Armando had plotted. I was still hot for Licha. But as a writer, or at least as someone striving to become a legitimate one, I saw this as valuable research. I figured to get a short story or magazine article out of an afternoon in a De Efe whorehouse. But Griselda acted suspicious. Maybe she sensed something in Armando's manner, or maybe she knew him only too well. Even after he and I were seated in the car and he'd started the engine, she lingered, leaning an arm on the roof and making idle chatter.

"It is such a beautiful, sunny day. I hate the thought of being inside."

"Then why not come to the Hipódromo with us, mi amor, as I suggested."

"No, you men want to be alone. We agreed. I would only intrude."

"You know you are always welcome, wherever I go,"

said Armando. "To the ends of the earth."

She stepped away from the car. "No, no, no. I should stay home and work."

"Well, whatever you think is best, my kitten."

Griselda glanced down to Armando in the idling automobile and frowned as if she had just gotten a whiff of the paper mill. Then she looked up and squinted at the sun. "Well, it is a nice day. Maybe I will go with you after all. If you two don't mind."

"Of course not. We are overjoyed. Come, my sweet."

As she walked around the back of the coupe to get in on my side, Armando looked at me and shrugged complacently. "Ni modo," he sighed.

At the racetrack Armando insisted on getting a table in the open-air clubhouse overlooking the final turn. We ordered cocktails and *la comida* from a white-jacketed waiter. Another came to take our betting slips and place our wagers. For a railbird like myself it was quite luxurious, with bleached tablecloths, crystal, and polished silverware. And the track was beautiful, with pink flamingos strolling about a lake on the infield. I suspected it to be somewhat beyond Armando's means, though he insisted on paying.

But luck was with me, and I was able to put him onto some winners going off at two-to-one and better, which more than paid for the outing. It had been the same on my previous trips to the Hipódromo. I suspected the Mexicans to be emotional, not scientific, bettors, playing lucky numbers or fetching names. Maybe some could not read *The Form*. Whatever, I saw to it that Armando came out in the black even after picking up the tab. Which was considerable given what he consumed.

He had apparently come off his diet. Before dinner he drank three tall *cubalibres*. Then he ate a meal consisting of soup, salad, roast lamb, fried potatoes, and dessert, a piece of flan, with coffee and brandy. But he was still hungry. He looked to his wife, holding his forefinger and thumb a millimeter apart.

"I'll get just a little more, my dear. I still feel a bit empty."

Griselda sat smoking. She glanced at Armando with heavy eyelids and went back to gazing at the flamingos and nursing a vodka-tonic. Armando called over the waiter and ordered a piece of chocolate cake. As he was finishing that we won another race. Feeling celebratory he ordered us more brandy and himself another piece of cake, lemon this time. Griselda sat and smoked.

The waiter returned with our drinks and placed the piece of golden cake, Armando's third dessert, in front of him. Eyeing it with obvious lust he lifted his fork. As he did, Griselda took a final puff on her Marlboro, reached in front of him, and pressed the cigarette out atop his cake, the red tip hissing in the yellow icing and turning black. Then she turned again to the flamingos.

Armando looked at his cake, fork frozen in midair. Then he lowered the utensil, pushed away the dessert as if uninterested, and, turning to me, shrugged. Ni modo.

*

That evening Licha returned to the apartment in a black mood. Her ex-husband had done his best to undermine her plans with their son, having arranged a children's party that left her little time alone with Alejandro. She paced from kitchen to dining room as if searching for an object on which to vent her frustration. I vowed that I would not be that object and hunkered with Armando in the living room. I had seen Licha angry before, had seen her blister those who crossed her with hot harangues, eyes ablaze, nostrils flaring, the trilled double Rs of her rapid Spanish sounding like machine-gun fire. Further, I had just awakened from a brandy-induced siesta and wanted to return to full consciousness in peace, with a mild kick-start from the coffee I sipped and some dark-chocolate toffee I'd bought at the track.

But just as I was reaching for the toffee, Licha stormed through the living room. She stopped abruptly before me and gazed down with eyes wide. "Chocolate toffee!" she exclaimed. "That is my favorite!"

I froze, momentarily speechless. But then I felt Armando's light touch on my sleeve.

"¡Sí! ¡Exactamente! That is what Rick said when he bought it for you: 'This is Licha's favorite. I will buy it for her because she too is so sweet and delicious. I have missed her so much all day.'"

Licha gazed down at me, tears welling in her eyes, a smile playing on her lips. "¿En serio? No, you didn't really say that, did you, Rick?"

Again I heard Armando's words sliding over my shoulder. "I swear to God, Licha, those were his exact words." Armando sat erect, right palm raised as if taking an oath.

I felt his hand release my sleeve. I grasped the chocolate, stood, and presented it to her with a kiss. She stared into my eyes and caressed my cheek.

As she devoured the toffee I glanced toward Armando. He winked and surreptitiously made a brief yet obscene gesture with his fist.

IV
Tu Esqueleto Es Vivo

After a week lying on my back reading Tolstoy, Turgenev, Simenon, and Katherine Anne Porter, I took a taxi back to the public clinic to have Dr. Ramos apply my walking cast as promised. Then I could at least limp up to the jardín and La Fragua. I could talk to people, enjoy the sun and the sunsets, and dine out with friends. And even if I couldn't dance at least I could drink and hang out at the clubs with Licha and Martina.

But when Ramos saw my ankle he shook his head and waved me away. "Not yet, gringo. The swelling has not gone down enough. Elevate it another week. Then I'll make your cast."

I could hardly believe my ears. Another week alone on my back in my dim cave while life passed me by. I felt as I had as a schoolboy forced to sit in a sterile classroom all day while outside the sun shone and birds sang. It brought back to mind the torturous imprisonment of a desk job. But there was nothing to do but submit.

I took a cab to the Biblioteca, then the only bilingual public library in Mexico, where I got a stack of history, fiction, and mysteries that the cabbie carried out for me. We stopped at a grocery where, using my crutches, I hobbled inside for a liter of good tequila and a bottle of cheap Mexican "bourbon." (In those pre-NAFTA days the protective duty on imported liquor quadrupled its price, making a bottle of Jack Daniels cost two weeks of Mexican wages.) Under the open-air *portales* on the jardín, where vendors positioned their carts, I bought four packs of Faros, the thin, oval, ribbed cigarettes that I smoked.

But I was still unprepared for what my second week of solitude would bring. Licha came once but left after only a few minutes. Taide, apparently trying to honor my privacy after her earlier intrusion, began preparing my afternoon meal in the kitchen of the casa grande and delivering it on a tray before quickly retreating. I had no other visitors except Martina, who stopped by for a few minutes on her way to work at the inn across the park.

One day, in order to get some fresh air and sunlight, I managed to hop up the twisting staircase to the barren second floor studio and sat on the small balcony watching children seesaw in the playground across the street. Two large black butterflies with brilliant yellow bands on their wings, Giant Swallowtails, floated by my balcony. They teased each other, soared in unison, parted, rejoined, and kissed. They pranced together up to the rooftop and down again to the cobbled street. But as they did, a young boy with a switch spied them and bolted from the park after them. With one swift blow he sliced in half the wing of one butterfly. It fluttered to the ground, where its wings futilely beat the earth. Its mate hovered over it for a moment then flew away, and I thought of Licha.

That summer and fall she had served as my guide on a strange, magical journey. Along with Jesús, Eduardo, Martina, Azul, Daniel and the rest of our group of friends, we lived with a verve and a hunger for life that seemingly affected and changed us all. Perhaps I was a catalyst, for I was the most hungry, both for experience and change.

Though still in my mid-thirties I felt like time was running out and that I had done nothing with my life. I felt like a man trying to catch the last train. To others it probably looked like I was happily drifting, but I knew better. Why then drop out and come to Mexico? I could not have answered that satisfactorily then. Something drew me that I did not clearly understand. Though now from a distance of some twenty-five years it seems clearer.

Of course there was a conscious suggestion, provided by my late comrade, novelist and photographer Bill Bornefeld. Years earlier he had lived in San Miguel de Allende, where, reportedly, he'd plotted a rebellion with the renowned Mexican painter David Siqueiros, who had even gone so far as to cache weapons for that purpose and who earlier had attempted to assassinate Trotsky in Mexico City. Also, I had vacationed in Mexico, in the capital as well as at Zihuatanejo. The clear air, bright colors, and warm people seemed a corrective for the gray skies and anxious Americans I knew. But what made me go to Mexico had more to do with my unconscious mind. I remember the moment it grabbed me and shook me, as if to make me finally pay attention to it.

Unless you have to be there, it's perhaps best to avoid St. Louis in the summer, when temperatures and humidity readings both reach one hundred. Same goes for winter, when natives pass weeks without seeing the sun, hidden behind low, gray clouds, and suicide rates soar. But bright, complaisant spring and autumn days arrive as transforming gifts. Particularly in the spring, when magnolia, cherry, and redbud bloom, and the air hangs moist and expectant with the smell of earth and blossoms. Nights come warm, clear, and comforting, enfolding you in a great ambient and starry womb.

On just such a night I drove west across Forest Park with the roof open on my Renault, letting in the stars, the moonlight, and the fragrance of magnolia. I'd just left Llywelyn's Pub after a satisfying evening of book chat and kvetching with my cohort Robert, among others, and headed to my twenty-first-floor studio overlooking the park.

Through the opened windows that lined the east wall of my apartment, Forest Park looked like a fairy-tale kingdom, with the spotlighted museum sitting atop Art Hill like a fortress, and the winding, tree-shadowed roads lit by yellow-glowing lampposts standing sentry-like.

I got another Heineken from the fridge—I'd lost count hours earlier of how many I'd had—and stepped out onto the balcony through the open door. I lit a cigarette and leaned my elbows on the cool iron rail, gazing at the boulevard below, where the headlights of passing cars lay fuzzy white lines on the dark street, like chalk marks on a blackboard. Even though the next day was Thursday I had no alarm to rise to. I did have a couple executive speeches I was working on, both with leisurely deadlines. Those two writing projects would pay me enough to spend a month in France. As soon as I finished them I was free to go. Free of a regular job, free of my ex-wife, free of confining relationships and obligations. I had a beautiful, privileged existence, everyone told me. Though I had my doubts.

I turned and walked back inside, passing into the alcove where my bed lay on the parquet floor. I took my keys from my pocket to place them on the nightstand. However, I paused, gazing at a framed cubist print from a Parisian gallery hanging above the bed, where my image, lit by moonlight, reflected in the glass. Then, apropos of seemingly nothing, I reached back and hurled my keys at the picture. The glass cracked at the point of impact and fissures radiated out to the frame. I stood there staring at my image, dissected by the fissures as though a man disjointed.

I had known it all along, it seemed, but without admitting it to myself: I knew I was wasting my life, and had grown into a man I did not much like. It was time to change, though at that moment I had no idea how, or into what.

So instead of traveling to staid, orderly France I soon set off south. Mexico seemed to offer a fecund, soulful existence at a time when life felt sterile and flat. I had sensed that in Mexico beneficent spirits lived, kin perhaps to those I felt vibrating from the earth as a child in the Illinois fields along the lake where we lived and Indian mounds still stood. But in my high-rise cell I no longer felt such earthy vibrations. So I went to Mexico to find that something that I had lost, even though at the time I had little inkling what it was and how to grasp it. Yet ultimately I found more than I could have imagined.

V
Gringos

Now in my second week of hibernation—still waiting for Doctor Ramos to apply my walking cast so I could once again immerse myself in the life of the *pueblito*—I saw that my sensory world had shrunken to a monotony of sight and sound: four walls and virtual silence, a physical existence lacking movement and sensory stimulation. My cerebral world was still there—my books, my writing, and my thoughts, which inevitably turned inside. Thus I was left, without diversion or society, to face myself, a much more wrenching task for a self-absorbed and self-critical gringo than a gregarious and self-loving mejicano.

But unlike some gringos in San Miguel, I had at least been alert and open to the novel culture and people around me as best I could. I was always listening—listening to the Spanish language and trying to comprehend its idiomatic syntax; listening to the stories of the hard, surreal lives of Mexicans; and listening to the tales of Americans. In Mexico nearly every American expat had a story to tell if only someone would listen. So I did.

Despite the sustenance I drew from the Mexicans I lived among, I needed to talk to Americans from time to time if for no other reason than to relax. Living in a language you are struggling to learn can be taxing. First, even the smallest need can produce anxiety and end in embarrassment. Once, at a stylish restaurant on my first trip to Mexico City, I put my cigarette out in a salt dish, having forgotten the word for ashtray and simply guessing or hoping that the lone plate on my table was it. Of course the waiter, being Mexican and thus by nature gleeful and expansive, had to point out my mistake to everyone else in the room so they could share in his mirth.

Second, unable to express nuanced thought in my newly adopted tongue, I felt as though my intellect had atrophied. Accustomed to examining my beliefs and musings by voicing them aloud, I at first spoke Spanish like a five-year-old, with simple, declarative sentences. I could ask for what I wanted but often could not say what I really felt or thought.

But a third and equally important reason moved me to seek out occasional gringo conversation. Although I was escaping America, I was searching for it as well, for my comforting childhood homeland that now seemed defunct. So in the stories of my countrymen I listened for clues and looked for signposts that might point the way home.

The stories of Americans generally differed from those of Mexicans, the latter's characterized by Fate, Disease, Death, Magic, and Miracles; the former's by odd dualities: Heroism and Indecision, Honor and Betrayal, Discipline and Self-destruction. Listening to Americans' stories helped me shape my own story and my own life, I realized, as I recounted them during my second week of forced solitude, frequently going to my journal to revisit or augment them. For in a life story compressed and edited to its essentials, you're able to perceive the structure of the tale and thus of the life. You can recognize the wrong turns, tragic flaws, catharses, and saving graces. You see where people screwed up or stepped up and did the right thing. You perceive how they might have altered their fates and how malleable our lives are. How, with hesitancy and misfortune or with good-will and good luck, a life can turn on a dime. I saw that my life too was mere clay, not a thing carved in stone, and that with my own hands and those of Fate it might be reshaped. That's what I learned by listening to my compatriots' stories.

Joe was typical of many older American men I met in Mexico. A veteran who fought in Korea, he was the sort of foursquare guy who followed orders, talked straight, and stood his ground. Yet that ground had recently been shaken by his wife of three decades who, apropos of nothing prox-imate, asked for a divorce. When Joe, incredulous, asked why, she answered:

"You kissed Mary first."

"What do mean?"

"When you came back from Korea. You kissed her first."

Joe shook his head as he told me his story over a beer in the shady patio of a dingy restaurant near the market. "You live with a woman for thirty years and you never know her. I was so stunned I couldn't speak. I just left."

He took a swallow of his beer and gave me the back-story: "After nearly three years overseas I got off the plane, and there beside my wife stood my two-year-old daughter I'd never seen. I dropped to my knees and hugged her and kissed her. Then I rose and embraced my wife."

A crow laughed in an avocado tree above us, and Joe looked up. So did I, not knowingly quite what to say.

*

J.D. Stinnet had another sad war story to tell but one with a happier ending. I can't remember where we first met, but we ended up at his apartment one evening drinking shots of *Geltwasser*, a sweet German liqueur festooned with flecks of gold, chasing it with beer to dull the cloying taste.

"This stuff costs $300 a bottle," he said as I moved to the john, "so use the strainer."

J.D. lived in an upstairs apartment at his uncle's house, up the hill in Atascadero, alongside other rich gringos and Mexicans. We watched the sun set red over the black mountains of Guanajuato, diaphanous clouds turning purple as J.D. told me his life's story. Recently, at age twenty-nine, he had resigned his commission as a U.S. Army captain. An exceptional choice for a West Point man and the son of a Cadet. But J.D. was exceptional in a number of ways.

His mother had died during his childhood. He was then orphaned when his father was killed in Vietnam. From a boarding school in Hannibal, Missouri, he went directly to the U.S. Military Academy, where he was granted admission as the son of an alum fallen in battle, and from there into the Army as a second lieutenant. However, not as a fighter but as a field surgeon. The map of his life lay before him, drawn by tradition and Fate. But Fate was not finished marking directions.

When Marxist hardliners overthrew the Grenada government and murdered Prime Minister Maurice Bishop in 1983, J.D. was among American troops that invaded to quash the rebellion. But what he saw there, and an aversion to the sort of American gunboat diplomacy that got his father killed, soured him on supporting such efforts. In protest he quit the Army. His father's brother, a former CIA operative, lured him to Mexico.

Trained to treat wounds and operate in the field, J.D. possessed skills well suited to Mexico. For in the *campo* lived peasants without the means, either physical or financial, to seek medical aid in town. So, under a United Nations program, J.D. went to them. He set bones and treated burns. He debrided infections and injected antibiotics. He delivered babies and brought advice. He laid on hands.

Assigned to work with him as assistant and translator was a Mexican R.N. who became his bride-to-be. She arrived at his apartment that evening when J.D. and I were in our cups, to drop off some well-appreciated food that she had prepared for us. Smiling and soft-spoken, she looked like a woman in love.

After she left I chewed a crisp *flauta* and said: "She's even more beautiful than I remember. You've got her glowing."

A smile played at the left side of his mouth. "When you met her before, we weren't engaged yet. That's to say…" He looked at the ceiling searching for words. "I've had to be very delicate with her. You see, she's petite. And a virgin. Or at least was. And I…Well, I'm gifted."

"Ah."

A military tradition that J.D. chose still to honor dictated that an officer have two best men at his wedding, a custom that seemed to signal a sort of expanded brotherhood: It said we're all comrades. That night he asked me to stand alongside his uncle as best man. As I walked home under a starry sky, I felt touched and honored by his request. But I was even more moved by his story, which suggested how unpredictable life was and how a man might, with courage and discipline, mark his own way, as I was trying to mark mine.

*

Another old soldier of San Miguel, David Gray, began writing a 1,400-page autobiographical novel at age 82. David had scores of stories, from the Pacific theater of World War II, from his hermit's life in Colorado mountains, and from small-town Mexico, where he had lived for years, moving back and forth between San Miguel de Allende and Progreso, on the Gulf of Mexico.

Despite his age David, a lanky six-foot-three, played tennis and drank a few beers each morning, walked up and down the steep hills of his adopted hometown every day, and even enjoyed a sex life, albeit serendipitously. I learned of the last when I went to his apartment one evening to watch the World Series on TV.

David rented a room from a well-to-do Mexican couple who had installed an enormous satellite dish on the roof of their new home in Guardiana, one of the ever-expanding *colonias* of San Miguel. He got a feed to his black-and-white set from the dish but had to watch whatever the landlord was watching. Fortunately, the husband was a Dodger fan and tuned in the World Series. However, if he left the house, his teenage son and twelve-year-old daughter would re-aim the dish to pick up the XXXtasy Channel. So David and I might be watching Fernando Valenzuela pitch a screwball then suddenly see Long John Holmes going deep.

However, this day David's sex life had not been so vicarious. I had dropped by earlier to check what time the game would be on but apparently missed him. Now when he opened the door for me the first words out of his mouth were, "Do I have a story to tell you!" As always, I was ready to listen.

He got us a couple Coronas from the fridge, and we settled back in front of the TV and a view of Dodger Stadium.

"Did I ever tell you about the little thief Magda from when I lived up the hill?"

I nodded. It was a bad thing. David had rented a cottage apart from the main house of a rich American widow, an ostentatious mansion with six-foot-high fireplace, marble stairs, and a grand piano. Some jewelry had gone missing, and the woman accused her teenage maid of stealing it. Shamed and distraught, the girl hanged herself. Then it was discovered the jewelry had been taken not by the maid but by Magda, the cook's daughter. The usual free-floating anti-gringo sentiment in San Miguel congealed into a near riot. At the suggestion of the police, the American widow left town with death threats hanging over her.

David went on: "I was sitting in the jardín after tennis, and Magda came up and sat beside me. I could tell she was just after some money, asking if I had any laundry or housecleaning to do. So I reminded her about the Polaroid camera she'd taken from me. She said that was when she was a confused teenager. Now she was twenty-one and had a three-year-old boy—no husband, of course—and didn't do that sort of thing anymore. Well, you know what a soft touch I am…"

"Yeah, ever since your arteries hardened."

"I told her I didn't have any housework for her but would give her some pesos to feed her baby until she found work. So we came back here to get the money, and I opened a few beers. She wanted to watch TV so I turned on the tube. And wouldn't you know it: The damn kids upstairs had the porno channel on—some couple banging away.

"I started to turn it off, but Magda was damn interested. Said she had never seen such things. Soon she was getting hot and running her hand up her dress. Which gets me turned on. Next thing I know I've got a hard on and I'm jumping on top of her. Can you believe it?

"I was going great guns, and then some asshole rang the doorbell. She jumped up for a second and before I could get it back in I lost concentration. She tried to help, but we just couldn't get the damn thing back up again…How about another beer? I feel like celebrating tonight."

I was happy to celebrate with David, although I did so guiltily. I didn't have the heart to tell him that I was the asshole who rang his doorbell that afternoon and interrupted what may have been his last at bat.

*

I found another American friend in the artist Arnold Schifrin, who understood the arcane rites of creation and divined the transformation I was going through, for he too had passed that way.

I had met Arnold at the hotel on the edge of town where I first stayed, when he came through San Miguel de Allende with a young woman. After knowing me but a few days, he suddenly said, as we drank a beer in the bar:

"You really don't see it yet in yourself. You don't know if you've got it. You're moving in that direction, but you don't know yet."

I stared at him. He couldn't have been more right. I had a thought, a hope, that I might become a real writer, that I might have a novel or something fine in me, a dream that had been buried under years of sloth, self-indulgence, and self-doubt. But it was just a dream, nothing I had yet committed myself to, for I was afraid to let go of my trapeze and leap for the next. By way of covering these fears, I said: "I know what direction I'm moving: toward the graveyard."

Schifrin studied me. "Ditch the callousness, Rick. It doesn't wear well on you."

Then, when he returned a month later, we bumped into one another on the street. He examined my face, gazed into my eyes, and nodded.

"Yes, it's coming. I can see the change. In the eyes: a warmth, an intensity, an improvement. It's coming."

But for Arnold, twenty years my senior, it had come decades earlier. He told me his story one night as we sat up late, well after midnight, drinking at my casita on the park. When I revealed to him how I made a living, freelancing commercial writing, he lifted his eyebrows and chin knowingly: "Ah, a hoor!" He knew, for he had been one too.

As a successful young dress designer in New York, Schifrin was making good money and living like a king. But one day he felt compelled to illustrate a poem and showed it to his boss. The boss took one look and said:

"Oh, what you want to be is a fine artist."

"What's that?"

The boss took him to the Metropolitan Museum of Art and stood him before a Rembrandt. "That," said the boss, "is fine art."

"Yep," said Schifrin. "That's what I want to do."

Despite the advice of his Brooklyn father to "paint on the weekends," Arnold quit his $20,000-a-year job (lots of dough in 1946) in favor of a $440 art scholarship. He locked himself in his studio and painted fourteen hours a day. For him, with work and discipline, it was coming.

But what Arnold believed he saw blossoming in me by now resided in him like a rock. He knew he was different—talented, ambitious, egotistical: an artist. His belief in himself as a rare bird who could do something no one else in the world could do, that is, paint his paintings, was an appropriate and necessary albeit, perhaps, elitist acknowledgement. Though it is a strange sort of elitism that compels one to choose poverty, isolation, and workaholism over luxury, fellowship, and ease.

To create true art one must live as an artist, Arnold argued in our long, late-night sessions. Forego the middle-class tethers and touchstones, the platitudes and complacencies; strip yourself bare; submit to an initiation that never ends, offering yourself up in sacrifice to the work. And one must always work, with great discipline and a constant searching for form. "The form is here in Mexico," he would say. "Study the form."

He encouraged me to immerse myself in Licha, whom he thought perfect for me, and in Mexico, which to him she personified. "Steep yourself in Mexico. All the questions are here if not the answers."

I had never heard such talk: vivid and direct, brimming with self-confidence and verve.

"I'm the man who can finish the whole fucking Mexican Revolution," he once said, speaking of the country's revolutionary painters. "There was Orozco and Siquieros and Rivera and Tamayo. I'm not Mexican, but I'm the one who can do it."

Orozco, he said, had made the great agnostic statement for Western civilization, doing with Man what Michelangelo did with God. The next day I went to the library to see what he was talking about. There I found photos of the Orphanage at Guadalajara, Los Hospicio Cabañas, to which Schifrin had referred. On the ceiling of the rotunda Orozco had painted not God reaching out to Adam investing Man with life, as Michelangelo had at the Vatican's Sistine Chapel, but two men desperately reaching out for one another yet never touching, forever frozen in a painful, godless solitude. The energetic darkness of Orozco's vision haunted me. Still today when I think of Arnold Schifrin I think of Orozco creating those bold, swirling strokes and remind myself to do the same. I see Schifrin painting twirling Mexican fireworks flaming the dark night as *mestizos* dance in their glow, a canvas as full of life as the man himself.

Once I was walking down the Cuna de Allende from the jardín when I heard a voice call, "¡Gringo! Hey, gringo!"

I stopped and looked around, but there was no one in the street.

"Hey, Rick! Up here!"

I gazed heavenward and there was Schifrin leaning over the roof of the Hotel Vista Hermosa, where he'd set up a temporary studio. With a brilliant blue sky and puffy white clouds as background for his trimmed white beard and impish smile, he looked like a mischievous God.

"Come up for a beer," he yelled down.

"Later. I've got a basketball game now."

"What are your team colors?"

"Blue and white," I shouted.

"No. Not good. Buy them new uniforms: red, for love." And he blew me a kiss.

*

One of the first men who befriended me in San Miguel de Allende had little interest in the earthy women there, being both ethereal and homosexual.

"Moses and the great prophets came from other planets," Sid told me during our first of many tête-à-têtes. That statement, along with his unwavering belief in reincarnation, his trust in the wisdom vested in tarot cards, his claimed extrasensory perception, and his active participation in a faith-healing group, established for me his credentials as etherealist. As for his homosexuality, I could only surmise (and credit rumors), for he never came on to me sexually, only intellectually and companionably. Besides, we were already old friends, he maintained, going back some three or four incarnations.

Sid carried a Mexican passport despite being born, like me, in St. Louis. His Mexican citizenship came through his "marriage of convenience" to the widow of his Mexican business partner. Sid provided for her and her young children; in return she cooked, kept house, and enabled him to renounce his American citizenship. This was perhaps Sid's way of traveling to another planet, outside the sphere where he was born, to become an official citizen of otherworldly Mexico.

"She sleeps upstairs and I sleep here," he told me, nodding at a daybed in the corner as we sipped rum with mineral water in his art gallery/office/study/boudoir.

His nominal wife was, however, a wizard in the kitchen. I remember fondly the kidneys in *jitomate* salsa she once served at comida. Sid, too, was interested in good food as well as literature and spirituality. Our conversations ranged from sweetbreads in white Bordeaux to Kafka to parapsychology.

He told arresting stories, true or otherwise, such as his meeting Eleanor Roosevelt and Diego Rivera's daughter, whom he described as "the two homeliest and the two most beautiful women" he had ever encountered. At other times we would sit comfortably silent for long minutes, sipping our *ron con Tehuacán*, letting the afternoon slide past.

Though of a serious bent, on his sixtieth birthday he turned gloomy. "There's no one for me to love," he said. "I love my adopted children of course, but that's different. Love is most important."

That day he spoke of loneliness, disappointment in others, and betrayal. Often when I passed his gallery where he sold Tarascan Indian carvings, I saw him at his desk playing solitaire or working a crossword puzzle, in a lonely world of his own making, which now seemed to oppress him.

Yet ultimately I think Sid came to feel betrayed by me as well. Perhaps he had thought that my interest in his comradeship indicated a kindred spirit when in fact it only indicated a writer, someone who conducted endless research, picking over the words and deeds of friends like a vulture over road kill. Perhaps he came to believe that I was just another one of the agnostic, egotistical, and heterosexual American bastards who had scorned him and driven him from his homeland. Perhaps, as I grew significantly cheerier—with Licha's help and the aid of all who had befriended me there—I was less prone to endorse Sid's dark pronouncements. Nonetheless, though our friendship had cooled, Sid wanted to read my tarot cards before I left town. So one afternoon I again stopped by his shop.

He had me cut the deck and laid out the cards in rows, the Emperor, Justice, the Knight of Cups, and the Knight of Wands in the first file; in the second a card depicting a boy and girl; in the third row the Pentacle, the King of Swords, the World, the Star, and the Tower; and in the final file a nude woman with flowing blonde hair.

The cards, said Sid, advised me to be cautious, but that my greatest fear, my entrenched self-doubt whether I could ever be a writer, would be overcome. And that I should not be ambitious or rush into things, advice I now wished I had heeded. My friends, he told me, would not always be supportive. He saw that my emotional life, as well as many other aspects of my being, would change. My two pivotal cards, Sid said, were the World and the Star, which meant that I would endure great struggle but that eventually everything I wished for would come to me, a prediction I cannot yet quibble with.

But I also realized that Sid was not so much reading the cards as reading me or sharing the wisdom of his experience, for I had heard much the same from him previously over rum-and-mineral-water. It was his way, I think, of giving me a parting gift, telling me paternally to watch my back, to bear down, to take my time, and to hoard hope. It was good advice, advice my own father might have given me, a gambler's creed.

With the tarot-card layout scribbled on the back of an envelope buttoned in my shirt pocket, I moved back down the street toward my rented casita on the Calle de Aldama. It was the hottest, dreamiest time of day: siesta. Everyone had just eaten their dinner and now lay in the cool darkness of their brick homes behind shuttered windows, dozing or making love.

As I picked my way on crutches down the narrow, twisting, cobbled *calle* I heard a child's cry growing. When the street bent, the cry came loud, and I saw its source: A boy of perhaps three had been locked between the curving metal bars of the bedroom window and its blue shutters. Behind the shutters, presumably, his parents made love.

As I passed I whispered to him: "Don't cry, *hombrecillo*. You'll have your turn someday."

At the time, the crying boy in his cage made me think of Sid, locked in a sexless marriage and embittered loneliness. But now, during the second week of my near-total solitude, I was experiencing hard loneliness firsthand.

VI
Living Inside Your Body

Though I had my stack of books, my mind began to drift when I tried to read. I'd spend most of the day simply lying on the banquette before the cold fireplace, left leg elevated, staring at the white ceiling. I guess I was meditating. I know I was wrestling with questions I had thus far left unanswered: What was I to do with my life? What sort of man was I?

I know too that I chastised myself: For wasting time. For lack of discipline. For the youthful and impetuous ten-year marriage that dead-ended. It seemed that I had made many bad choices, running down blind alleys with my work, with women, with everything. Nothing I had ventured had yet borne fruit.

But as the week progressed and my meditations ultimately focused on the piquant existence I had fashioned with Licha and my Mexican friends, I came to see that I had in fact accomplished something over the years, albeit nothing to put on a résumé: I had struggled to live right and find my own path. If in hindsight I now saw that I'd made some bad choices, so what? They had at least been honest choices, playing the cards I'd been dealt. I'd followed my heart and my hunches, using whatever limited knowledge I had had at the time. I saw I wasn't near perfect and never would be. I was human. And if I fell short of abstract gringo codes of morality, honor, courage, discipline, and efficiency, ni modo. In order to fully embrace life I needed to jettison the guilt and self-chastisement for past failings, to forgive myself my shortcomings past and future, like a good Mexican. I saw that I needed to change who I was, to nurture the best parts of myself, and that, with fortitude and time, I could do it.

This came to me that second week not with a thunderbolt and inscribed tablets proffered from above, but in a quiet, infectious Mexican manner, precipitated by my musings on my countrymen and Mexicans, on Licha, Ernesto, Martina, and all the others who had befriended and beguiled me. Their example was intoxicating. They all lived in the here and now. Today, this moment.

I had often heard Mexicans say of Americans: "Gringos do not live in their bodies," but I had no idea what they meant. Now I thought I did. For I too had been a typical gringo guilty of this transgression against nature, of living not in my body but in my mind: rigid, logical, logocentric, moralistic, self-critical. I'd lived a life of images, symbols, words, thought, and abstractions. Even my joys and diversions were largely cerebral and passive: books, films, writing. I had to an excessive degree been a mere spectator of life.

But now as I lay motionless in my dim, airless cell, it became clear to me: The greatest pleasures and satisfactions came not from symbolic life but from real life, from the direct experience of the senses, that is, from living in your body. Pleasure came from nature: from food, drink, lovemaking, companionship, movement. From dancing and from running on the basketball court, from viewing orange sunsets and vermilion flycatchers, from inhaling the scent of flowers and perfume. From the gratification of your own animal body.

Most Mexicans seemed to know this intuitively, as if a birthright. Always ready to sing, to dance, to drink, to toil, and to rest, whatever their bodies told them. But this was more than mere hedonism: It was vital and vivid life. They were showing me by example that the portals through which I must pass to reclaim myself parted not with words, no magic "open sesame," but through movement. Through submission to my animal nature and through reverent appreciation of the rich material gifts given us. Maybe that's why Mexicans indulged themselves so much in the contemplation of Death, as a reminder of the precariousness of sensuous existence.

I saw the magic life I'd lived in Mexico. Dancing with Licha to soft salsa, her perfume wafting to me, then strolling arm-in-arm through the cool, quiet dark to my bed, where Nahuatl chants floated from the park on night air, sliding through the shutters to caress us. Beneath blue skies walking cobbled streets between half-millennium-old walls, and through the markets past stacks of chiles, frijoles, and exotic fruits. Smelling the cut roses, the burros, and tequila; savoring the scent of cilantro, cardamom, and cinnamon winging to me from somewhere on a mountain breeze. Watching the people: the dark smiling women with their beatific children, the stoic men of dignified mien, people who paused to genuflect when they passed a church and who'd share with you their last tortilla. Eating spicy meats under the portales with farmers come to market, downing cool beer and savoring Oaxacan tobacco with Ernesto at La Cucaracha, running with my teammates on the court in the *parque*. Mexico had penetrated me, seeping into me like a balm.

Both Licha and Martina set seductive examples of self-love and self-forgiveness. The day after some excess they were always incredulous that they could have behaved in such a debased way. It was as if they were speaking not of their own acts but those of some incorrigible kin whose on-going misbehavior could not be emended, as Martina had when she came by to visit me that second week. She arrived with flowers in one hand and the other to her forehead.

"What's wrong?" I asked. "Hangover?"

"No, worse," she said. "A moral hangover."

She explained that the previous night, after a substantial amount of tequila, she'd had sex with Lázaro, a married saxophone player.

"Why did I do such a thing, Rick?"

I reminded her, perhaps indelicately, that she had done such things previously.

She grabbed me by the shoulders and stared into my eyes as if I had revealed some deep hidden truth. "Yes! I can't help myself. It's crazy!" She released me and lit a cigarette. "Ah, well. There are worse sins."

Likewise with Licha. Whenever she showed her haughty, arrogant side, which was not infrequently, she dismissed it without self-reproach. Once, I dragged her to a movie in the run-down Aldama cinema. She sat silent, glaring at the screen throughout the entire film, the story of disenfranchised South Americans fighting to overthrow a cruel dictatorship. I thought she was mad at me for insisting on this passive pastime when we could be dancing, drinking, or making love. But when we emerged from the theater, she exploded:

"Why don't they ever make films from the dictator's point of view? Why are we made to feel sorry for the *pobres* in the barrios, who are sheep that deserve whatever they get."

I told her: "You, Licha, are a spoiled brat."

She lifted her chin. "Yes, I am special."

*

A seeming male counterpart to Licha, Daniel, or Novedades, served as an instructive example of living in the moment and inside your body. His fluid, sensual life gave support to the local saying that San Miguel had no whorehouse
because with all the gringas in town there was no need.

A strikingly handsome and bilingual young man of
twenty-five, he worked as night manager at the same hotel
as Licha. But his nickname spoke to what truly occupied
him. Time and again I'd see him about town with a different
woman on his arm: at La Fragua with a comely middle-age
Chilean woman whose lawyer husband worked in De Efe;
at Laberintos with an eighteen-year-old daughter of a New
York publisher; at a quiet restaurant with a septuagenarian
English widow. Thus he was called "*Novedades,*" a Spanish
noun meaning "novelties," which certainly described Daniel's ever-changing partners, but which also could be broken
up into the sentence, "No ve edades," or, "He doesn't see
ages."

It was perhaps to his credit that, democratically, he admired and romanced teens to grandmothers, dancing with
them, staring into their eyes across a dinner table, making
love to them. I recall once spotting a lovely young American
girl sitting on his doorstep at three a.m. awaiting his return
after I had just spied him at Mamma Mia's dancing with a
woman twice his age. To some people he likely appeared
only a callous gigolo. The truth, I suspect, was more nuanced that.

To his credit, he always answered to his nickname. For when sober, he was always jocular and full of high spirits.

"Oye, Novedades. ¿Como estás?"

"Regular, amigo. Muy fucking bien, my friend."

San Miguel de Allende Spanglish carried a certain playful currency among bilingual Mexican and gringo residents, with conversations often borrowing creatively from the other language or simply slipping back and forth between the two. The American writer Hal Bennett, who hadn't left Mexico for twenty-five years, spoke to me in a witty bilingual hash whose appreciation required extensive knowledge of both languages. Novedades, too, spoke this whimsical San Miguel Spanglish, which he used in his work, both as hotel manager and gigolo.

Mexicans have an aphoristic pun about languages: The best way to learn a tongue is with saliva. I suspect Daniel was a good teacher. But his language skills coupled with his bonhomie made him a good comrade as well. He was always ready to buy a drink, tell a story, or prowl the bars looking for romance. Or simply to pass a pleasant hour with you sitting on a metal bench in the jardín, admiring and complimenting all the women from seventeen to seventy who passed by.

Yet Novedades apparently carried a torch for his Chilean beauty, for whenever her husband was out of town he paid her special attention. I'd see them walking hand-in-hand through the streets, or at comida together in the flower-strewn patio of the Posada Carmina, or dancing cheek-to-cheek at Laberintos. They made a lovely couple. That is, until he got pummeled in the street late one night.

I barely recognized him when I ran into him in the jardín.

"¡Daniel! ¿Qué pasó?"

He squinted at me through puffy black eyes and spoke out the side of split lips, his swollen jaw barely moving.

"Dos noches ago yo estaba en the street en frente del Ring, bien drunk. Two hombres—yo no sé who—came up from detrás. Kicked mis nalgas and stole mi Swiss reloj. Y dos cientos pesos also."

A mugging in the streets of San Miguel was a rare occurrence indeed. So rare that his story didn't set quite right with me. You'd even see little old English ladies, the sort Daniel might romance, walking safely through the jardín at midnight, little English flashlights in their hands. My first thought was that the Chileña's husband had corrected Daniel or that he'd gotten into a fight over one of his other paramours. But that wasn't it at all.

When I next saw Licha I asked: "What happened to Novedades?"

She rolled her eyes. "Drogas."

"¿De veras?"

She nodded. "Trouble with the narcotraficantes. They want the money he owes them for cocaine, but he doesn't have it."

"What will he do?"

"I told him to ask his Chilean friend for it. But he said she's already been very generous."

"Maybe he should leave town," I said. That was always my solution to problems, no matter what town I was in.

Daniel did in fact soon disappear. I hoped he'd left town on his own accord to find a safe hamlet where the local drug pushers wouldn't find him and was not simply escorted by the *narcotraficantes* to a shallow grave in the campo. At the time I did not sense the always lurking, sometimes lethal dangers of Mexico, and when I did I denied them. I was trying too hard to live to worry about death, figuring to outrace it.

*

Drugs also played a role, albeit indirectly, in breaking the heart of my friend Javier. Perhaps I too played a part but, I think, a minor one. His story demonstrates a potential risk in living life open-throttle, with Mexican hope and bravado, always following your heart. Yet it was a risk most Mexicans seemed prepared to take.

Javier and Heather were in love in a way Licha and I were not. Young love. Holding-hands-and-making-plans love. She came from Ohio, as I recall. Javier came from Querétaro. She was eighteen, he twenty-two. Her parents were rich, middle-class Americans financing their teenage daughter's summer wanderings in dubious Third World countries; his parents were poor, middle-class Mexicans who were happy he was supporting himself although, by American standards, marginally.

Javier worked at a tourist agency booking flights and hotel rooms. He drove a used Volkswagen Beetle that he kept polished and lived in a small apartment down the hill near the Tuesday market, where Heather had moved in.

Despite their differing backgrounds they looked like they were made for each other. Both were short, sandy-haired, and freckled yet attractive. He played in the basket-ball league on a rival team and played well. She was taking courses at the Instituto Allende, Spanish and water colors. They lived frugally but happily. Licha and I would see them at the disco on locals' night dancing, smiling, sitting at one of the low tables with their heads together as if making plans.

They were in fact plotting on spending their lives to-gether. I didn't know their exact plans, but from what I knew I could fill in the blanks: They'd marry so he could get his Green Card and work in the States while she finished college. Then she'd put him through school. They'd work and save their money and return to San Miguel to start a business, something to do with tourism, most likely, and to begin a family.

I can imagine a young man, or any man, making such plans. Before meeting her, your life has seemingly turned up a blind alley. Then suddenly there stands a door, a portal through which you can escape into a green, sunlit Paradise with a beautiful young woman who is your fated life's partner. Your existence now becomes a glowing dream, and you live off love and hope in an intoxicating present that invokes an Edenic future. But then comes the serpent.

San Miguel can seem like Paradise to Americans, particularly at first. The air is clear and warm; the pastels of the colonial houses vibrate in brilliant mountain sun; the Mexicans are gracious and helpful, your expatriate countrymen hospitable and intriguing. A wealthy gringo from, say, rainy Seattle or snowbound Toronto might be so thoroughly seduced as to lease or even buy a spacious home in Atascadero after but a few weeks. You would see this gringo around town for two or three months drinking and laughing at La Fragua, taking courses at the Instituto, turning tan, maybe even falling in love. With this always-younger Mexican lover at his or her side, the gringo or gringa could then be seen dancing at Laberintos, swimming in the thermal waters of Taboada, or dining at La Princesa. Then one day you might spy the Mexican lover alone or with someone else and ask about the gringo(a)'s whereabouts.

"Se fue," you are told. He or she went. And you never see the northerner again.

For the next year or two the house in Atascadero stands vacant except for the maid, whom the generous American owner hired in perpetuity and who now treats the grandiose mansion as her own personal clubhouse. Sometimes, if you are observant and quiet, you can learn of possible reasons for the owner's sudden departure, little things that could build to a crisis: Workers stealing. A lingering case of dysentery. Mexican friends who fail to show for dinner. Trouble with the past tense. A mosquito in the bedroom. A dose of the clap. A long, lonely weekend. A series of bad hangovers. An angry, bilingual confrontation where some local pulls a knife and threatens assassination. Soon the gringo is searching for the cockroach in his salad, looking over his shoulder when he staggers home at night, and longing for his true friends back in Seattle. But other times it takes just one incident, if of sufficient magnitude, to send someone packing.

One day near noon as I sat in the jardín—as sanmiguelenses called their town square—taking the sun and watching the people pass, Heather approached and sat beside me. Generally San Miguel was a town of happy people. Particularly those lucky Mexicans and gringos who had nothing better to do than enjoy the sun, take the waters, or laze about the jardín. So, unhappy people were conspicuous. And one look at Heather, who was most always gay and smiling, told me she had joined the latter group. She bit her bottom lip, and her hands shook.

I gazed up at the sun and said, "Nice day," in hopes of deflecting any unhappy speech.

"Rick, can I talk with you?"

"¿Cómo no?"

"I mean confidentially. I don't want Javier to know because I'm afraid of what he might do."

I leaned back into the shade of the elms. I suppose Licha and I treated Heather and Javier somewhat paternalistically, particularly Licha, offering to stand in for her mother at the wedding and teasing them about their obvious mutual affection. As a result, perhaps Heather viewed Licha and me as mature and worldly. Maybe that's why she had come to me for advice. Or perhaps she had nowhere else to turn.

"Sure. What's wrong?"

She bit her lip again. "Do you know Vicente?"

Although I frequently saw him about town, I knew Vicente only in passing and had worked to keep it that way. He owned a popular restaurant and seemed a popular guy. But when I first looked into his eyes, I saw something ruthless and conniving. Later when I heard rumors that his restaurant was financed with drug money, I was not surprised.

"I know him well enough."

She looked up from her shaking hands. "Do you think he's friends with the drug soldiers? I mean, could he actually get someone in trouble?"

I took in a long breath and thought, Oh shit. "Tell me what happened."

"Well, he's been giving me some dope…"

"Marijuana?"

"Yes, just marijuana. But now he wants me to sell it to my friends, to other Americans I know. I told him I couldn't sell drugs. He said I had no choice. If I don't do it, the drug soldiers will arrest me and plant drugs on me. Can he really do that?"

Heather did not see the rich indigenous irony in her situation. It was very Mexican. If she sold illegal drugs, she would be protected from prosecution; if she refused, she'd be arrested for trafficking.

"Hell, I don't know. But why risk it? Maybe he can sic the drug soldiers on you, whom I doubt would treat you with respect."

She stared at me, perhaps picturing that disrespect. "But I just can't do it. I can't use my friends like that. I can't be a drug-pusher."

More irony: a drug-user who denigrates the drug-seller.

"I'm saying that you don't have to, and you don't have to go to jail either. I'm saying choose door number three."

"What's that?"

"It's simple: I'll walk you down the hill to your place, help you pack, and put you on the next bus to De Efe. There you'll catch a plane and be back home with your folks tonight or tomorrow."

She shook her head as if I was being absurd. "I can't leave just like that."

"Why not? School starts again next month. You'll arrive just in time."

"But Javier…"

I waved away her concerns. "Don't worry about Javier. He loves you. He'll follow you anywhere. You two were planning on going to the States sooner or later, weren't you?"

She looked down past her shaking hands and sat staring at the stones beneath her feet.

Heather didn't let me walk her to the bus station but did soon leave town, and left Javier behind.

When I saw him on the basketball court he told me he would visit her in Ohio at Christmas and meet her family. Her father, a lawyer, was arranging a Green Card. Javier was still happy, for he was living in that idyllic future that he and Heather had planned. But then he started deteriorating. I could guess what happened. Anybody could.

Since he had no phone and she lived in a school dorm, it was hard to talk. At first he got letters almost every day. Then he got none for a week but chalked it up to the spotty Mexican postal service. Good news was on the way he told himself.

But in her next letter Heather seemed distant and businesslike, talking of her classes, not of their happy plans. Two weeks later, in her final letter, he learned that she had decided to devote herself to her studies for now and that the Christmas visit was off as her parents were taking her skiing.

Javier stopped smiling. I'd see him driving his Volkswagen past the jardín, gazing straight-ahead, somber, looking neither left nor right for friends who might want to chat. On the basketball court he played with a ferocity I had not before seen in him. One day he got into a brief yet stupid fight over a foul call and ended up with a black eye.

I know nothing of what became of Javier or Heather over the years. Maybe they are both living happy lives, wherever they may be. But I wonder if either is as happy as they were that summer.

However, thinking about them and their parting as I lay on the banquette with my left leg elevated made me wonder whether I was kidding myself about the healing powers of Mexico. At times the two cultures, Mexican and gringo, seemed to touch only tangentially, as if confined within impenetrable borders. Yes, I found the Mexicans' eccentricities refreshing and their folkways fascinating. But I sensed I was just skimming the surface. I wondered whether, like Heather, I would someday soon return north and abandon all that had once seemed so vital.

VII
Movement

After my second week of solitude I once again had Taide call a taxi and rode to the public clinic on the north side of town. The ankle was still badly swollen, and I feared what Dr. Ramos might say. The prospect of spending yet another week in solitary confinement darkened me. As much as I may have profited by my isolation, enough was enough.

But when Ramos saw the ankle he merely shrugged. "Good enough," he said. "Let's put the cast on."

"Great."

He spread his hands. "Where is it?"

"Where's what?"

"The cast. I need materials to make a cast. This is a clinic not a pharmacy," he explained.

He told me what he needed and sent me down the block on my crutches to a *farmacia*, where I bought the necessary wrap and cement. I tottered back, the ubiquitous Mexican bolsa, the pastel plastic sack offered with any purchase, swinging from my crutch handle. I had come to appreciate the Spartan Mexican pharmacies, with their window displays of trusses and ointments. First, you could get almost any medication without a prescription, even drugs whose unauthorized possession in the States could land you in jail. Second and more important, if you had a headache you could walk in and order two aspirins and a bottle a Tehuacán and not have to purchase a hundred pills and a six-pack of Perrier like you did in the States. The Mexican economy was predicated on penury and scarcity, not on affluence and surplus like back home.

When I returned to the clinic Ramos applied the cast.

"There. Finished."

I stood, looked down at it, and frowned. My ankle was fixed at an angle so that only my toes touched the ground.

"How can I walk on this?"

"You can't. You'd need a walking cast."

"I thought that's what you were giving me."

"There are no prosthetic heels in the whole state of Guanajuato. I checked just yesterday for another patient. This is the best I can do."

I feared it wasn't good enough. I'd already fallen twice trying to negotiate the cobblestones on my crutches.

I asked how much I owed him. Again he shrugged.

"Whatever you think is right. Bring me a bottle of Cognac…You got a cigarette, gringo? Good…Hey! I thought I told you to stop smoking."

*

Dr. Ramos has remained an enigma to me. I wanted to get to know him better, to hear his life story, to pick his brain. But he was too elusive for that sort of direct, gringo-istic approach. Thus he continues to appear to me like an expressionistic jigsaw puzzle with key pieces missing.

Once he showed up at a cocktail party carrying a valise and dressed in the olive-drab jumpsuit he wore when piloting his Cessna, along with crash helmet, sunglasses, and boots. He asked the hostess if he could use the bath and disappeared into it. Half an hour later he emerged showered and clean-shaven in a coat and tie. I watched him as he sat at the small bar across the room, quietly downing drinks. After perhaps three brandies he jumped up.

"My God!" he exclaimed. "I have to call home. My wife will think I crashed!"

Like his camouflaged, multi-antennaed German jeep, his airplane seemed an extension of the man, inseparable from his image thanks to stories, true or not, of the Flying Doctor's inept navigation. I was told that one colleague, whom Ramos was flying into San Miguel de Allende from a hospital at Guadalajara, glanced at the gas gauge that read empty and asked, "How much fuel do we need to get to San Miguel?"

Ramos answered, "Twenty-six minutes."

"How much do we have?" the passenger asked, staring at the needle resting on E.

"Don't worry. The gauges are broken. Let me figure."

Ramos computed with a pocket calculator taped to the ceiling of the Cessna. Finally he announced, "We have sixteen minutes fuel," and began looking for a level spot to land.

He apparently did land safely that time but was not so fortunate later, I had heard. Upon flying into the Querétaro airport he reportedly spied a stunt plane that infatuated him and talked the owner into letting him fly it. After a series of loops and dives Ramos misjudged a maneuver and crashed the plane into the ground yet walked away unhurt. In compensation for the demolished aircraft he gave the owner his Cessna, a plane he had sold to his brother the previous day, and took the bus home to San Miguel.

My friend Jennifer, who had recently divorced and moved to Mexico from Washington, D.C., with her two young children, took her four-year-old son to Ramos. The boy had had plastic tubes inserted in his ears at Homer G. Phillips Hospital in D.C. to guard against frequent ear infections. Ramos took one look at the devices and pronounced: "Take those things out. You are just inviting infection."

After Ramos had examined the child and written a prescription, Jennifer asked how much she owed him. Ramos shrugged but said nothing. She told him she needed a written bill to submit to her insurance company. He nodded and left the room. Five minutes later he returned and handed her an invoice.

She stared at it and said: "But this is blank."

"Put in whatever you like," he suggested, "and when the insurance company pays we both make money."

"I can't do that," Jennifer protested. "It's not honest."

Ramos gazed about his flyspecked surgery—at the broken window, the cracked leather of the examination table, the decades-old instruments—and spread his arms.

"This is what honest gets you."

Once, Ramos cured my friend Ed George of some malady and won his admiration. As they sat chatting and smoking cigarettes in his surgery, Ed told him, "You know, you're really a good doctor. You should be director of this clinic."

Ramos rose halfway out of his chair. "I was! I was!"

In payment for his services, Ed brought Ramos a set of intercoms he had purchased for him in De Efe. When Ramos saw them he broke down and cried unashamedly for minutes, tears streaming down his face. Finally he looked up and said, "I do not deserve it," and waved Ed out of his office.

Neither Ed nor I ever discovered the reasons behind Ramos's tears or his fall from grace at the clinic. In all things he remained a mystery.

*

As I recuperated, Taide brought me fresh flowers each morning, washed my dishes and clothes, made my bed, boiled my drinking water, and sought my command. Whenever I requested anything of her she nodded and answered: "Para servirle"—in order to serve you.

However, in Mexico, unlike egalitarian America, to serve another did not carry the same stigma but almost seemed to confer honor on the servant. Of course such cultural norms were propagated by those being served. Yet near daily I encountered seemingly gratuitous acts of kindness, that is, people serving me or others.

Of course most service sprung from poverty and powerlessness: the boy who lugged home my groceries to earn a few pesos, the seamstress who sewed me tailored shirts from white homespun cotton for but a few dollars, the old beggar who blessed me whenever I pressed a coin into her hand, or the wiry campesino who carried firewood into town on his burro and stacked it at my hearth as if arranging an offering to the gods. As someone who materially, culturally, and genetically had more in common with the Spaniards who subjugated the aboriginal peoples of Mexico than the mestizos and *indios* who served me, I surely benefited from my dollar-based status in this postcolonial Third World country.

Yet, for all the cruelty and bloodshed that informed the Mexican past, the people lived in the present, within the sphere of their own circumscribed lives. And within that world, despite whatever horrors helped shape it, they seemed to live with a generosity of spirit that, as an urbanized gringo, I found quite foreign. A postcolonial theorist could make a good case implicating me in the ongoing exploitation of these sons and daughters of both Montezuma and Cortés. My luxuriating ease came about thanks to Spanish swords, the excesses of the Inquisitors, the guns of U.S. Marines who invaded Vera Cruz in 1914, the virtual (and at times literal) enslavement of workers in the fields of Oaxaca, and ongoing international capitalist domination. One could speak of entrenched hierarchies of subjugation and exploitation grounded in the Church, the Spanish class system, transnational corporations, and even cruel, lingering Aztec shadows, which combined to disempower and mute the Mexican subaltern, i.e., the lumpenproletariat peoples who washed my socks, hauled my groceries, fetched my cocktails, and swept my gutter. But that would not explain the human warmth one encountered everywhere in these dispossessed people.

Their motivations seemed largely communal and spiritual, not material. How else to explain their hospitality, their interest, their concern, their unbidden aid? So often in a Mexican home, people who had little to eat shared it with me. They sought to hear my story and to tell theirs. They helped me up when I fell. They gave me gifts and sought my counsel. They'd lead me miles just to show me a newborn goat or a startling sunset. They prayed and sought God's blessing for me.

Their lives were often hard beyond my full comprehension. But invariably their response to toil and deprivation was thanks for small blessings, a hopeful smile when for a moment their struggle eased. They seemed to sense that the hard history and fickle future were givens about which, voiceless, they as individuals could do little. Their response was not to curse their fate but to praise the rare instance of beauty. It seemed to me a wise choice.

Still, class and class-consciousness always lay just below the surface, seething, both among Mexicans and between Mexicans and gringos. The valorization of things Spanish and the denigration of things "Indian" marked Mexico, despite the fact that most Mexicans had at least some Indian blood. This led to a strange dance of self-loathing and denial that seemed unnecessary to an outsider from a more heterogeneous and less rigidly stratified society. I learned not to ask middle-class Mexicans about their aboriginal ancestors, for often even those with, say, obvious Mayan features would claim to descend from full-blooded Spaniards. I heard even educated Mexicans patronize the short, dark, campesinos as *chaparritos*, the little people, and tell what they thought to be amusing anecdotes about the ignorance and unsophistication of these peasants. On Mexican television, which I usually saw only in passing when in the capital, the personalities seldom looked Indian but, rather, European, with blonde women holding a special cachet. Significantly, the cynical slogan of one of Mexico's leading lagers, Superior, was "Su rubia"—your blonde.

But there was more than self-mocking humor in this pervasive class-consciousness. I saw a vicious fight break out between local "*rústicos*" and arrogant young chilangos who came from the capital for a fiesta. Commonly I would witness campesinos—particularly the older men and women, those who perhaps still remembered the conflict fomented by the Mexican Revolution and the literal slavery that it ended—I would see these short, dark, leathery country folk step off the sidewalk and into the gutter to let me, whom they likely perceived as a señor, a lord, pass unmolested and untouched by them. I learned too that many of the most brutal soldiers and policemen, the ones who tortured and terrified the powerless Indians, often came from that same underclass, their violence seemingly signaling self-hatred and self-abnegation.

In San Miguel de Allende the presence of some two thousand gringos raised the class tensions even further. For we were the rich and powerful barbarians who claimed the best homes, ate at restaurants most locals could not afford, and slept with coveted women like Licha. Further, Licha's vivacity and European visage, tall, pale-skinned, and slender, exacerbated the situation. In fact, she had so little Indian blood that she could have been on Mexican TV. My maid, Taide, after having once chatted with Licha, told me, "Your girlfriend speaks Spanish very well," thinking she was a gringa.

Licha's blithe arrogance worried me. She seemed not to notice the eyes of Mexican men watching our every move at La Fragua or Laberintos. If she let her hand drift to my thigh or belt buckle, symbolically slapping the face of any

Mexican man who impotently looked on, I quickly moved it away. She remained unconcerned when men, such as Pablo, muttered "Malinche" as she passed, equating her with Cortés' Indian mistress.

"Pablo is just joking," she said.

But I knew better. I had noticed Pablo watching her. I had seen his eyes tighten when once, in her cups at Laberintos, she made a salacious remark about fellatio. I also noticed that he never addressed me or looked at me in Licha's presence, at least not that I saw. Then one night at Laberintos shortly before I left San Miguel, his seeming envy and hatred boiled over.

That night Licha, Martina, and I were joined, fortunately, by Ed George, who saved me from what could have been a beating or worse. For I was still on my crutches and could barely stand without them, much less defend myself.

When we arrived near midnight the disco was packed, so we joined a table of Licha's friends, Pablo included, in the back, behind the bar. I arrived in a good mood—although I couldn't dance, I could drink and had had a few at La Fragua. But clearly Pablo felt not so lighthearted. He sat unspeaking at the opposite end of the low table, glaring at me with crazed, dilated eyes.

Soon he rose and moved to Licha, who stood behind me, whispering to her and pushing her away from me. She, however, made light of whatever he was telling her—she too already half-drunk and feeling festive. Pablo turned to me and mumbled something incomprehensible, leaning into Ed, who sat next to me. Ed rose abruptly and knocked Pablo back, apologizing as if it had been an accident. I thought the two of them would fight. But Pablo simply shuffled away, moving off into himself, resuming his seat at the far end of the table and continuing to glare at me.

I glanced at Ed and said: "He's all fucked up."

"Yeah, he's on something. Watch yourself."

"Well, I can always beat him with my crutch."

"Don't worry about it, Rick. I can handle him."

I knew that Ed could, though you would never guess it by looking at him. Tall, thirtyish, bespectacled, long-haired, and well-spoken, he looked like a trendy young professor. Though American, he had grown up in Spain, where his father had been a diplomat. He held a black belt in karate and carried a stiletto in a sheath sewn inside the denim jacket he always wore. Once, at the train station in Querétaro, he held it to the throat of a Mexican who, with the encouragement of two amigos, had tried to mug him. Ed addressed the other two with his Castilian accent as he knelt on the chest of the mugger, whose legs he had kicked from beneath him: "Take your friend away now, or I will kill him."

But this night, despite Ed's reassurances, the tension that Pablo generated was enough to suck any fun from the evening. Then he flipped a lit cigarette across the table. It bounced off my chest and lay smoldering beside my drink. Pablo gazed at me challengingly. But I had no visible or vi-able response. Later that night I noted the moment in my journal: "Here I am, a civilized man, having to deal with drug-crazed neurotic assholes who want, perhaps, to see me dead." But I really didn't know how to deal with him.

Ed, however, seemed to relish the opportunity to respond. He plucked the hot cigarette from the table, holding it lengthwise, the filter on his thumb, the glowing ember pressing against his forefinger, and stared deadpan at Pablo as if impervious to pain. This bit of intimidation, Ed told me later, was really quite painless if you happened to have been holding an icy drink for some minutes beforehand. Then he put the cigarette to his lips, puffed on it, folded it into his mouth with his tongue, and pretended to chew and swallow it, smoke streaming dragon-like from his nostrils.

His tricks seemed to give Pablo pause. Nonetheless Ed leaned to me and said: "Maybe we should go. If a fight breaks out, everyone will be pulling knives, and who knows how many friends he has. More than we do."

Licha, who was at the bar, had remained oblivious to the drama. When I explained to her why Ed and I were leaving, she looked me up and down questioningly then said: "Bien. But I will stay and dance."

"And I will live to dance another day."

*

Within a week I decided to leave town but not because of Pablo. I had fallen twice more, both times after a tequila or two. Further, Licha had turned somewhat distant and cool, apparently still angry with me for breaking my ankle and disrupting her social life. Then I ran into a German madwoman who offered to drive me to the border, though she didn't seem insane at the time. When I found out how truly troubled she was, it was too late. Luckily she was not overtly suicidal when our lives were in her hands.

Let's call her Kirstin, just in case she is still alive, which somehow I doubt. I was introduced to her one day at a café on the jardín. Blonde, slender, fortyish, and stylish with a fetching German accent, she rented a house in San Miguel but lived primarily in Texas with her psychiatrist husband. In fact, she was leaving for San Antonio in a few days and looking for company on the long drive.

It felt like synchronicity. I knew I had to return north soon, as my money was running out. But I dreaded the prospect of taking the bus back to Mexico City and getting to the airport on my ill-wrought cast while carrying two bags. This seemed the perfect solution. Kirstin would pick me up at the door of my casita and deliver me and my luggage to the San Antonio airport. From there I could catch a flight to St. Louis, relying on Red Caps and baggage handlers to move me and my things about.

Suddenly everything began falling into place. The day before I left, Ernesto came by with a cane from his shop. I would have to leave my borrowed crutches with Taide, and Ernesto's gift was just what I needed. And that evening Licha, not the cool and distant Licha but the old, enamored

Licha, dropped in for a good-bye kiss. Afterward, as we lay abed, she lit a cigarette, blew a cloud of smoke in my direction, and, leaning on her elbow, studied me.

"You cannot leave."

"¿Por qué no?"

"Because I am pregnant."

"No, you are not."

"I could be."

"Todo es posible."

She tried another tack: "Why are you leaving me? Now who will I sleep with?"

"No sé. That is not my problem."

"No, but it is a big problem for me. How will I ever replace you? Maybe I never will. ¡Ay de mi!" She took another drag. "Nonetheless, I will begin looking tonight."

I shook my head. "You are a piece of work, Licha."

"Yes, I am special."

I brought her hand to my lips. "I'll come back."

"Promise?"

"I promise."

"Then I will wait for you. But write me before you come, so I can kiss all my lovers goodbye."

"I will be sure to do that."

"Go on! Go back to those gringas! But no one there will make love to you like I do and tell you that you are beautiful."

"No, no one there will tell me that."

"That is a lie! There will be hundreds of women. I know those gringas. They tell a man anything to possess him. Ay, Rick, you never should have come."

"I had to. All was fated."

"You truly think so?"

"We were meant to come together. Do you remember the night we met? You put your hand here when we were sitting side by side in the bar."

"Me? No. Impossible. I would never be so bold." She lit another cigarette from the pack on the nightstand and stared at me. "Well, maybe…Yes, that sounds like me."

*

Next morning Kirstin came as arranged, punctually, at five. She drove a sleek, black, Japanese coupe. We headed out over dark, narrow roads toward San Antonio, fifteen hours up the highway. She moved the car deftly through tight turns in the looping roadway. A mist hung over the valley, shimmering in our headlights. On a straightaway I glanced at the speedometer. The needle held steady at ninety-five.

She wanted to talk. I liked to listen. Within minutes I learned that over the past year she had survived two earnest suicide attempts. Once, she had shot herself in the chest with a rifle, just grazing her heart. "I'm usually a good shot," she complained.

Next she had tried pills and was saved only when her husband came home early to find her unconscious. After a stomach pump and a week in a coma, she was her old self.

I asked: "How you doing today? Good?"

"Oh, yes." She dismissed my concern with a flick of her wrist. Though I wished she'd keep her hands on the wheel.

As we rode north across the high desert she told me her life story, or at least some version of it. Not only was I unsure how reliable a chauffeur she was but also how reliable a narrator, for much of it seemed torn from an implausible novel. Her father, she said, was a missile scientist for the Nazis. When the Allies began bombing Berlin, he had their large, white house painted black to make it a less obvious target. Eventually she was smuggled out of Berlin in a coal tender.

Her relationship with her husband, as she presented it, was odd, to say the least. She told me of rifling his briefcase to find a lurid diary of an affair. Secretly Kirstin then copied his office keys and there found the name of his paramour in his papers. She went to confront the woman. While the two were talking, Kirstin's husband telephoned his mistress, and they invited him over for a drink. "My husband is a psychiatrist," she told me, "but he understands nothing of women."

Though people like Kirstin perhaps defy understanding. She told me of how she entrapped her husband, who was a virgin, into marriage. And of seducing her boss, with whom she had a five-year affair, even going on vacation with him and his wife. I looked again at the speedometer and made a silent vow to keep the chatter light and cheery all the way north. I did, in fact, elicit from her at least one lighthearted story—in her eyes—on the protracted trip.

While sunbathing topless with her twenty-year-old daughter within the walled garden of her San Miguel home, Kirstin retrieved her camera to take a picture. Focusing the telephoto lens, she noticed movement just above the wall. There, hidden amongst the leaves of an avocado tree, perched the neighbor's gardener, staring down at Kirstin's daughter and masturbating.

I laughed along with Kirstin despite being saddened by the tale. I identified with the gardener, both as a man who admired often unattainable beauty and on a symbolic level. Were my dreams just that, unreachable fantasies? Would my passion fall infertile—unacknowledged or derided? Was I merely masturbating metaphorically when I imagined myself capable of becoming an artist? And now I was returning to my mercantile native land, where I would necessarily shunt aside such esoteric questions and quests and join in the seductive yet demeaning commercial melee. There, I feared, my dreams would atrophy, and I wondered if I would ever return to Mexico. I wondered if I would ever find myself.

PART TWO

VIII
On the Street of the Lost Writer

I brought the brown-bagged half-liter of tequila to my lips, sipped, and returned it to the leather satchel on the carpet between my right boot and the cast on my left ankle. A woman wearing a business suit, sitting across the aisle in the San Antonio air terminal, glared. But I really needed a drink. After months in Mexico without telephone, television, and notable noise, my skin had thinned. I felt under attack by the beeping electric carts, the scraping flight announcements, the booming music from a nearby bar, the shouting passersby. Advertising on walls, magazine racks, TV screens, and T-shirts assaulted me.

Conversely, in San Miguel there was little to sell and thus little inclination toward salesmanship. As with the proprietor of the hardware store where I walked one day with the painter Arturo, who needed a small hammer to stretch his canvases. The man said he had none.

"Yes, you do," said Arturo. "There, hanging on the wall behind you, is exactly what I want."

The owner turned, gazed at the hammer, and turned back. "But that's my last one. If I sell it to you, what will I display?"

I had come to accept such un-American inefficiency. You learn to shrug when your waiter, whom you haven't seen for half an hour, returns now wearing a jogging suit. You come to relax and enjoy your solitude when friends stand you up. Finally, you endure with good grace and good humor the challenge of negotiating ancient cobbled streets and steep hills on homemade crutches when no prosthetic heels exist in the state of Guanajuato.

Yet now I was returning to my more efficient, business-like homeland. Here I would necessarily join the salesmen and hawk the one commodity I had left to sell: myself. But I knew I shouldn't complain too much. Despite whatever other failings, America was great for making money. I'd plunge back into it holding my nose and knock down fifty bucks an hour freelancing while back in Mexico my team-mate Efrín, point guard and La Fragua waiter, supported his family on fifty cents an hour plus tips. While my friend Hernán, a Mexico City literary critic, sat trapped in De Efe by Third World economics, unable ever to study in Madrid, where he could ill afford to travel.

So I told myself not to whine. With a little luck I could save enough in six months to return to Mexico for another six. Even compared to most of my own countrymen I enjoyed a privileged existence. I remembered the tedium of my Teamster days, hustling freight on truck docks to pay for college; the stress-filled, sixty-hour weeks as a newspaper reporter and editor; the angst and boredom of my three aberrant years as corporate hack. I reminded myself of the father of four pulling third shift at a Flint, Michigan, brakeshoe factory. But my heart kept luring my thoughts back to Licha's lithe body swaying before me to soft music, to her warm flesh moving against mine, to fresh mountain air and red sunsets, to the smells of cilantro, patchouli, and sweat.

Over the months Mexico had infected me. Now I glowered at the thick Americans who passed before me in Bermuda shorts, disdainful of their demonstrativeness, their garishness, their loud voices. Even the hissing sound of their language, all the esses of English, seemed to forewarn me, suggesting a tangle of vipers. I had returned from a land of adults—soft-spoken, decorous, somber-clad people—and landed in a seeming adolescent madhouse. I felt I had made a mistake, however unavoidable, and reached again for the paper sack.

From the loudspeaker came a boarding announcement for my flight to St. Louis. I replaced the tequila bottle in the leather satchel, positioned it on my lap, and maneuvered the wheelchair past the disapproving woman in the business suit.

*

In St. Louis I went to a doctor to have my cast cut off, carrying along my Mexican x-rays. He took a look at them and said: "I see no fracture here."

After paying him fifty bucks, I had seventy-five dollars to my name, which I blew in East St. Louis clubs my first night out. I hadn't planned it that way. But once I got partying I figured the worst thing to do, karmatically speaking, was to hoard such a paltry sum. Better to scatter it about like magic seed, hoping it might sprout and grow over-night—which it did, in a way.

Next day I telephoned a colleague and patron at a PR agency who, coincidentally, had just received a call from a deep-pocketed client with a crisis. Within two hours, clad in pinstriped suit, I was sitting in on a brainstorming session with a team of lawyers, engineers, and other flacks figuring how to control damage and plot a counterattack.

The crisis, I recall, had to do with alleged impropriety in the awarding of multimillion-dollar engineering contracts for the new metropolitan light rail system. But I was barely there, unable to focus on all the minutiae of corporate credentials, bidding procedures, and political intrigue. Rather, I was in Mexico, Licha lying fragrant beside me in the gathering night, the clacking of boat-tailed grackles piercing the shutters as the birds winged to their nightly perches in the jardín.

After the meeting, burdened with an armload of files, I returned to my studio. Still dressed in my suit, I lay on the bed in the alcove, staring at the white ceiling. I needed to get to work. I had news releases and backgrounders to write for the next day's press conference. But I lay gazing at the ceiling for an hour, maybe two. No thoughts, no movement, no nothing, as if in a coma.

Finally I sat up, thinking of the Buddha and The Noble Eightfold Path: right view, right resolve, right speech, right action, right livelihood, right effort, right mindfulness, right concentration. Number five, right livelihood, always tripped me up. I knew this sort of deadening endeavor was bad for my soul, but I saw no easy way out. The money came fast and bought me time to read, to write, to travel. It would enable me to change my life, I told myself. But in my heart I knew it was also holding me back, impeding my transformation.

*

After nearly a year of freelancing I headed back to Mexico, debts paid, apartment sublet, and enough money to live frugally for perhaps another six months. I traveled eagerly although, as always, with apprehension. Despite my familiarity with Mexico, each time I returned I was shocked, for it was always like slipping into a dream. As much as I anticipated the vibrant colors, piquant aromas, stoic people, and sense of primal mystery, whenever I reentered the country I felt as if I'd taken a good dose of ether, fallen unconscious, and was dreaming it all.

The bittersweet surreality was everywhere and unavoidable. On the plane I sat next to an elderly Mexican wearing a Jalisco straw hat, a man who'd been visiting his daughter in Houston. As we approached Mexico City he asked me in an odd, halting Spanish to read to him his customs declaration instructions, claiming bad eyesight. Then, when he asked me to fill out the form as well, I realized he could neither read nor write, and spoke as mother tongue an indigenous dialect perhaps never written.

As the plane touched down at the capital, I glanced out the window to see a dog, one of the country's ubiquitous pariahs, loping across the runway. Only in Mexico. It reminded me of the lively Mexican song that everyone danced to and sang at the disco, the Fucking Dog Song:

> Chingue perro, chingue perro, chingue perro,
> chingue perro, chingue perro.
> Chingue perro, chingue perro, chingue perro,
> chingue perro, chingue perro.

So went the chorus. That followed by a staccato middle-eight:

> ¡Chingue, chingue, chingue perro!
> ¡Chingue, chingue, chingue perro!

But my return to San Miguel de Allende came not as I had envisioned it, not as a return to Edenic peace and camaraderie but rather as another immersion into sterile isolation and loneliness. Licha had moved back to Mexico City to be near her son. Martina had gotten involved with an alcoholic American musician and was not her old carefree self. Ed

George had returned to his wife in the States. Ernesto was nowhere to be found. Most evenings I sat alone at La Fragua, drinking watered-down brandy—until I complained.

Sitting at a low table in the lounge by the cavernous, cold fireplace, I ordered a Don Pedro straight up from an indifferent waiter who had ignored me for five minutes. After the first sip I called him over again.

"Has any water been added to this brandy?"

"Claro que no. No es posible."

"Please bring me another."

The second was just as watery as the first.

"This is obviously watered down. Taste it."

"No. Es solamente brandy derecho. Espérame. I will show you."

He soon returned with a bottle of Don Pedro and poured me a stiff one. I sipped.

"Ah, this is the real thing."

"Es lo mismo."

"No, it is not the same. Look…"

I held the two glasses up side by side. The last drink was noticeably darker.

The waiter lifted his chin. "Ah, that is because the first drink was not Don Pedro but Presidente, which is less dark. There is no charge."

I looked him up and down and turned away. Apparently I had stumbled onto some hustle he and the bartender had going, stealing liquor or receipts. Thus he now became suddenly solicitous, bringing me more mineral-water chasers on the house without my even asking. Once he came over to adjust the ashtray, moving it two inches closer to me. At first arrogant, self-confident, and dignified, the man now seemed to shrink into an obsequious servant, presumably afraid of being ratted out, losing his job, possibly ending up in jail. But I decided against saying anything to the owner, Rafael. Instead I left a large tip, figuring I had developed a relationship that would assure me honest liquor in the future.

*

I was staying at an inexpensive hotel, actually an old colonial residence, near the jardín while I searched for a suitable apartment. I had enlisted as my real estate agent one-legged Juan, a middle-aged sanmiguelense who hung around the jardín and swung around town on a homemade crutch. I sometimes shot billiards with him at the Club de Deportivos, a seedy joint near the market where working-class Mexicans gathered to drink beer and play cards at metal folding tables.

At other times, usually late at night, I'd find Juan lying in the street dead drunk. Once, I alerted the next beat cop I saw, in hopes that he would help Juan home or move him somewhere he'd be less likely to get run over. The cop moved off lethargically in the direction I indicated, but I never knew if he did anything to help Juan or merely added to his misery by kicking or arresting him.

However, I soon learned that Juan had a poor aesthetic

eye as real estate agent, finding only dark, joyless apartments in arid, treeless courtyards. So I remained domiciled in my hotel room.

One night I was awakened by a fluttering about my head. At first I thought I was dreaming but then felt something brush by my ear. I sat up straight in bed and switched on the lamp. A dark movement drew my eyes upward just in time to see a large bat disappear above a ceiling beam of the five-hundred-year-old house.

I looked at my watch on the nightstand: 3:30 a.m. I took a swig from the water bottle there, but my mouth remained dry. I stared at the spot where the bat had disappeared, feeling suddenly chilled. I had no intention of lying down under the blankets again, turning off the light, and waiting for the bat to begin sucking at my jugular. So I pulled a worn armchair into the bathroom, closed the door, and managed, after an hour of stomping on cockroaches, to get a few hours sleep. I dreamt that the bat had been sent to punish me for some transgression but was unable to determine what it might have been.

I checked out of my hotel, disputing the bill with the dueña, who insisted I pay for the whole night despite my being able to use the bed but a few hours. The bat, she said, was analogous to a mosquito.

"Sí," I responded, "it too will suck your blood."

She rolled her eyes and walked away.

In the jardín I found Juan, who looked even puffier than

usual. I told him I needed a place to stay for a few nights, any affordable place, until I could find a suitable apartment where I could settle in for six months.

He looked at me and pursed his lips. "Do you have a peso?"

I handed him a coin, and he moved on his crutch to the pay phone under the portales. After a few minutes he returned and gave me an address on the lower side of town: 13 Calle Margarito Ledesma.

"Un apartamentito," he said, "en una casa grande. Muy bella."

I nodded dubiously, given my previous real estate experience with him. But at this point I was desperate and not about to sniff at poor aesthetics.

"Whom do I see there?"

"La dueña, a very nice American lady, from Texas."

"Ho boy," I muttered under my breath.

"Go after midday. She will be dressed by then."

*

After a breakfast of eggs with jalapeños at the Café Colón, I went to the library to await my appointment with my prospective landlady, Señora Peggy. From a 1946 Harper & Bros. reference book, *A Treasury of Science*, I learned that the vampire bats of Latin America, *desmodus rotundus*, often bit sleeping humans "on the under surface of their toes." This they could do stealthily, without waking their victims, thanks to their own soft feet, on which they would creep. That bite would start a flow of blood, aided by an anti-coagulant in the bat's saliva, which the animal would then consume licking with its tongue, not sucking the blood, as was popularly believed. With twenty-inch wingspreads and bodies the size of a rat, they hung head downward by one leg when resting. Capable of transmitting paralytic rabies—the thought made my toes curl—they often returned to an old wound on the same animal or human. But their bite was usually painless. Without the blood stains the next morning to alert them, few victims would realize they had been bitten.

Though I had no way of knowing whether my night visitor had been a desmodus rotundus or more benign species, I shivered at the thought of returning to my hotel room, one of the few in town that I could afford, and resolved to take whatever Señora Peggy had to offer.

As I strolled down the Calle Margarito Ledesma my thoughts were on the writer for whom it was named and with whom I felt a certain kinship. For years Ledesma, an aspiring poet, had sent unpublishable poems to editors and found only well-deserved rejection, I'd been told. But then something happened. His awkward verse suddenly took wing and soon found an audience. With numerous publications, he became one of Mexico's most popular poets. But he could never be found, legend had it, and his royalties piled up in an untouched account in his name. Though no new work from him had appeared for years, some Mexicans

I met believed that Ledesma was still out there somewhere writing his poetry.

(The truth, however, was more prosaic. Two decades later I discovered that Margarito Ledesma was in fact the pen name of Leobino Zavala, who died in San Miguel de Allende in 1974. Described by critics as an "involuntary humorist," he was known to family members as a very funny man who wrote comical poems for relatives' birthdays.)

Whatever romance attached to the name of Margarito Ledesma, little could be found on his namesake street. I could not tell much about the home Juan had sent me to, as it sat behind a twelve-foot-high white brick wall with the ubiquitous broken Coke bottles embedded in concrete atop it. Across the street sat another wall, this one yellow, with four-foot-high black letters spelling out "Bardahl." Through the open gates of the Bardahl Lubrication Center I could spy—among blackened oil drums and stacks of old tires—cars and trucks waiting to be greased. On the opposite corner sat a makeshift mechanic's shop, concealed hardly at all by a three-foot-high stone fence. The yard there was littered with derelict automobiles, discarded automotive parts, and greasy motors hanging by chains from tripods. Lean, piebald dogs slunk among the debris. Soon, after moving in across the street, I discovered that the shop also spray-painted cars and trucks in the yard, sending noxious fumes wafting over the neighborhood.

The doorbell at my new home hung in limbo, in typical Mexican fashion, from two wires, awaiting its affixing to the newly painted wall. I reached up to press it and was knocked back by a surge of electricity that ran up my arm and down my spine.

The bell sounded, and I waited. After a few minutes I reached again for the bell, this time careful not to touch the exposed wires. But still no one came to the door. After a third cautious ring I retreated back to the town center, thinking of my casita on the park where I had lodged the previous year—where birds sang, the air hung moist and fragrant, and Licha and I made love.

*

After two more futile trips to the Calle Margarito Ledesma, the door finally opened in early evening and I met Peggy, a weathered, sixtyish, oft-widowed woman from Waco, I was to learn. Her home, a new, one-story construction, surrounded a bare earth patio on three sides. No trees had yet been planted, no flowers bloomed, no water flowed in the central fountain. She showed me the room she had available but seemed wary of me.

"This is only temporary, until you can find another place," she said. "I was looking for a lady companion, but Juan said you were trustworthy."

Yes, Juan could trust me to pay for the beer and the billiards and to rat him out to the cops when he littered the street with his truncated corpus. Nonetheless, I noted how my Mexican status had sunk: the drunken, one-legged street hustler was *my* character reference.

My room had been designed as the maid's quarters, but Peggy, hermit-like, employed no servants. The size of a walk-in closet, it contained a narrow bed, a lamp on a warped wooden nightstand, and an inhumane straight-backed Spanish chair seemingly inspired by the Inquisition. But more noteworthy was what the room lacked: a desk, kitchen, or closet. However, there were four nails driven into the stucco wall, sufficient for hanging my few clothes. A lone window the size of a medium pizza had no screen or curtain. On the whole, the room embodied all the ambiance of a jail cell, albeit with the bathroom hidden behind a communicating door. I saw immediately that it was a place to sleep and little more.

But what I did not immediately recognize was that without a kitchen I had no way to boil drinking water. And with no *tienda* for long blocks in my quasi-industrial neighborhood where I might buy bottled water, difficult to keep enough on hand. The untreated tap water of San Miguel de Allende, I had learned by hard experience, seemed specifically formulated to avenge Montezuma against foreigners. So, to keep from getting dysentery via the indigenous water-borne bacteria, I went to a farmacia for a bottle of iodine and would put a drop or two in a plastic quart milk-jug of tap water. While it killed the bacteria, it tasted like hell, and after a few weeks of it I felt certain I was poisoning myself or had developed stomach cancer, for I endured near-constant abdominal pain.

However, my stay on the Calle Margarito Ledesma was leavened by Peggy's hospitality. After her initial wariness had waned, she often invited me into the main house for bottled water and conversation. She loved to praise good books, denigrate the Mormons, and expose family secrets. I learned that her mother had conceived her out of wedlock and thus had to get married at age forty. She also told me of her uncle, a successful opera singer forced to quit the stage when he lost his teeth (exactly how, she did not say). He next became a Denver motorcycle cop until a debilitating traffic accident ended that career. So he retired to Majorca, where he could afford to stay drunk and where he was buried. Along the way he married and divorced three times. When he divorced his third wife, Peggy said, his son married her a week later.

*

Prior to my late-night encounter with the bat in my hotel room, I had never given bats much thought. But now they appeared everywhere, as if having long waited offstage for their cue.

Javier, the cab driver who moved me and my bags to my new address on the Calle Margarito Ledesma, laughed when I told him why I was changing domiciles.

"You cannot escape them," he said cryptically.

He was right, in a way. Though I had never before noticed them, now they were everywhere. At night I saw them winging above the streetlights, devouring mosquitoes. In the jardín or at the *mercado,* the distinct Spanish word for bat, *murciélago*, would frequently flutter to me, and I'd turn to its utterer as if homed in by radar. With most everyone I now met, the conversation somehow turned to bats, including stories of country kin who had been bitten and bled. In a stack of recently donated books at the library, I came upon a Batman comic. A Batman movie came to the Aldama Cinema.

Then at the Bellas Artes—a nunnery reinvented as art museum and gallery that I had visited on a half dozen occasions—I was drawn to a large, aged mural that somehow I had never noticed but that now gave meaning to the rampant *murciélagismo* all about me. In the foreground two white-homespun-clad campesinos, one on horseback, strove to lasso a great, black, man-sized bat that hovered lecherously over three señoritas cowering in its shadow. A romanticized pueblito sat in the background, a Mexican Socialist's dream village, with swept streets, plumb walls, and white-washed homes, like none I'd ever seen. I was so struck by the mural that I noted it in my journal, describing the painting as "a beautiful illustration of macho psyche, protecting innocent womanhood from the menacing, animalistic, phallic darkness." I wondered if it had been painted by a priest or, perhaps, one of the nuns who had inhabited the old convent.

I felt a newfound identification with nuns and priests, for I was living the life of a monk in my bare cell on the

Street of the Lost Writer, eschewing sensual pleasures and mortifying my flesh with iodine water. My cloistered, high-desert existence made me long for waters, for woods, for green expanses and movement. At night I dreamt of lakes and lush meadows. Still I could not turn tail and return north, which held little other allure and limitless angst. Neither could I admit that Mexico no longer held healing magic for me.

*

I saw that no matter how much I may have profited by my previous trip to San Miguel de Allende, my journey had just begun. Life once again seemed arid, a feeling exacerbated by the shadeless sterility of my lodgings on the Calle Margarito Ledesma. To avoid lingering there, I spent long hours at the library, in the jardín, walking the hills, and stalking the bars. But my spiritual dryness could not be quenched. I quickly shunned those I met, all of whom, Americans, Canadians, and Mexicans alike, seemed only to grate on me.

Emblematic of San Miguel's lost magic was the Coca-Cola promotional truck I spotted making door-to-door deliveries, as if supplanting the milk truck in Mexico. It moved through my working-class neighborhood with music blaring from loudspeakers on its roof, young girls running to front doors with bottled Coke four-packs, dispensing cultural poison, I felt.

It was in such an unhappy state that one night after supper I sauntered down the hill toward La Cucaracha, a seedy cantina on the low side of town. I had looked into La Fragua and Mamma Mia's in hopes of finding some ambient life, but the former was too dead-still and mausoleum-like, the latter too noisy and gay. It seemed that nothing could break my black spell.

In the street outside the cantina I heard laughter and jukebox *ranchera* music. I sidled through the baffled doorway and there, standing stiff at the bar as though thoroughly drunk, amid a crowd of revelers, was my alcoholic, wetback-running compadre Ernesto. When he saw me he threw his arms up in the air, sloshing a uniformed soldier standing next to him with beer.

"Rick! Where you been you crazy son bitch?" he called in English.

We embraced, and Ernesto began to introduce me to his friends. The fact that I was Ernesto's comrade immediately ingratiated me with the band of drinkers. The soldier Moises, who was even more *borracho* than Ernesto, pulled me aside to say that if I could provide him some marijuana, he would see to it that I would never have problems with the drug army. Ignacio, a hulking drunk taller than I, said Ernesto was like a brother to him and offered to strong-arm my enemies. Patricia emerged glassy-eyed from the back room, where a dice game was underway. Ernesto introduced us then whispered in her ear. She slid an arm around my waist and said she and her girlfriends would keep me entertained as I long as I stayed in San Miguel.

Next I met Alberto, who made his living selling electric shocks to macho drunks in cantinas and who offered me, as a friend of Ernesto, a free demonstration. He had me grab in either fist two metal handles attached by wires to a homemade hand-crank dynamo with voltage meter. As Alberto ground the generator, all gathered round to see how much juice I could take. I stood amid the circle of drunken mestizos, my hands going numb and my arms tingling as the voltage grew, the band urging me on: Ernesto laughing and drinking, Patricia smiling licentiously and licking her lips, Ignacio giving me a thumbs-up, others hooting and cheering. I felt a sure charge pass through me, electrical and electric. I was back. Mexico was still surreal and seducing; Mexicans still joyous, wild, and endearing; and I felt once again ready to take it all in.

IX
Complete Liberty

The next morning I swallowed down a couple aspirins with iodine water and made my way out through the metal gate, moved past the yellow Bardahl wall and the snarling German shepherds within, and headed toward the jardín. As I trudged up the dusty Calle Margarito Ledesma and turned onto the Calle de la Aurora, a little girl perhaps five-years-old carrying a plastic sack of canned goods raced past me on the stone *banqueta*. But as she approached a cantina ahead, she tripped and fell on her face. At that moment a drunk staggered out the cantina's café doors, stepped over the sprawled child, and muttered to her in passing, "¡Ándale!"—travel on.

When it happened I thought it a good omen, signaling that all was *regular*. For whatever deprivations Mexico engendered, no matter how fucked-up things got, there were always the Mexicans with their wry acceptance of life's pitfalls. It was a hard country, but of its many assets—its silver, gold, oil, pristine beaches, and fertile land—its staunch people were its greatest treasure.

I had coffee and eggs at a small café on Calle Umarán then went to the grocery store on the jardín to check the bulletin board where people posted handwritten ads selling unneeded baby carriages, seeking transportation to Texas, and offering furnished apartments. I spied a neatly printed bilingual notice that had not been there the previous day: Small furnished apartment in "un jardín tranquilo." In my mind I saw the garden and shaded lakeshore of my youth, the Eden that was my first world. I reached up, removed the thumbtack, and folded the ad into my shirt pocket. I knew intuitively that I had found my home, a home I would return to year after year, as if reuniting with my second family in my second homeland.

I marched past the post office and up the Calle de Correo to a door but two hundred yards from the jardín and rang the bell. I followed the dueña, Señora Guadalupe Martinez de Gonzalez—Lupe, as I would come to call her—through her unkempt garden. A portly retired schoolteacher, she walked limping, with a cane. Her mannish features, histrionic facial expressions, and girth would combine in most to make for a plain woman. But once you glimpsed her essence, from that day on your eyes played tricks on you, as if a spell had been cast, and you saw only a beautiful and vital creature.

She showed me a small studio, once perhaps servant's quarters, off the patio at the rear of the house. A single room ten-by-ten: semicircular brick fireplace in the corner, a bed, a wardrobe, a desk, and a chair, with barely enough space to walk between them all. Cool stone floor. A kitchen with glass doors, no bigger than a closet. A bathroom/shower with a drain in the center of the floor where, I discovered, scorpions liked to lurk at night.

Outside teemed her jungle-like garden: figs, avocados, and limes; pomegranates, papaya, and poinsettia; lilies, bougainvillea, and jasmine. A homemade ladder led to the roof, where I could watch the sun set pink over the dark, distant mountains guarding Guanajuato and harvest avocados that thumped the roof at night. In other words, the place was virtually perfect.

I asked Lupe, as delicately as I could, in the most formal and oblique Spanish I could muster, if one might entertain guests there. Despite how much the place felt like home, I was not ready to rent a monastery cell, figuring that sooner or later my monkish ways would wane. Sensing my meaning, Lupe laid a cool hand on my wrist, gazed at me with raised eyebrows, and whispered as if in conspiracy: "Libertad completa."

In the kitchen of the main house I met Lupe's raven-haired daughter, Naomi, then in her twenties, who spoke English and helped conduct business. When my cash-in-hand fell short of the required rent, I offered to walk down to the bank and return with it in minutes. Mother and daughter exchanged a few rapid words. Naomi turned to me with raised palms.

"That is unnecessary. Simply bring it when you return with your things. My mother trusts with her eyes."

I turned to Lupe, who sat with her hand resting on her cane, her eyes resting on me not so much in scrutiny as in welcome.

*

One of the few souvenirs of Mexico that I retained over the years is a *cajita*, a small wooden box with clear Plexiglas front. The size of a paperback book, it's painted deep orange and trimmed in dark blue. Through the plastic window one can see a sugar-sculpture skeleton with sombrero pushing a tiny wooden wheelbarrow down a cobbled street. Next to him stands a paper cutout of an elegant young woman in a blue dress. Beyond her, three drunken cardboard campesinos pass around a bottle of tequila. The backdrop consists of a picture postcard of a San Miguel street, the pastel pink cathedral, La Parroquia, looming in the distance. This diorama, this cajita, is representative of a whimsical and witty Mexican art form. On the back, in dark blue ink, the artist has inscribed: "A Rick: Una calle cualquiere del pueblo Escondido. Beatríz." The night she gave me the cajita was the last time I ever talked with her, for soon afterwards, keen on self-preservation, I made a point of avoiding her.

I'd run into her at La Fragua one evening during my

hermitage, as I called it, my withdrawal inside the walled garden of my new home on the Calle de Correo. Most days I passed sitting in the jungle reading and writing. Lupe would at times join me, once bringing sweet-smelling jasmine in a vase for my room, another time fresh pulque from the campo. She'd sit on a stone bench across from my sling chair, her cat Quiquo, black with white boots, lying in her lap, and comment on her plants and flowers, rue the changes come to San Miguel or Mexico in general, and discuss with me global economics, Mexican politics, and human nature.

A ladder-backed woodpecker often drilled at a tall pine just on the other side of the whitewashed wall as if to punctuate our pronouncements. Yellow-rumped warblers and vermilion flycatchers looked down upon us from tamarind trees as the scent of *limón* wafted across the garden, making the things we discussed seem even further away. Lupe moved with her cane about her walled sanctuary, amid pale green ferns, red *nochebuenas*, blooming *azucenas,* and fragrant fruit trees, watering the plants and supervising Chucha, a toothy, cadaverous Indian woman who came from the campo twice a week to clean and do laundry, the latter accomplished by hand at the concrete scrub-board and sink hidden in a corner of the patio. The sun most always shone in blue skies, the magenta bougainvillea seemed to pulsate, and iridescent green hummingbirds buzzed about. I felt as if I had never left Mexico and, in my heart, probably hadn't. This was real life, I perceived. My cold, gray, cerebral existence up north, which I had originally carried back to Mexico with me, now seemed surreal, like a bad dream. I felt as if I had come home, and secluded myself within the high, white walls of my miniature Eden, indifferent to the world outside.

Also living there, in another small apartment at the back of the garden, was a thirtyish British painter, a drugged-out-looking bloke who called himself Colin Weatherby. But Colin was seldom around, spending most of his time with a well-to-do Mexican woman in Morelia who was bank-rolling an exhibition of his work in the capital. Nor did I see much of the blonde woman who had taken an upstairs apartment on the other side of the garden. So I retained my relative solitude.

I passed days and evenings largely alone except for oc-casional conversations with Lupe, the waiters at La Fragua, drunken cowboys at La Cucaracha, or, in rare instances, Ernesto, who proved more elusive than promised. My soli-tude was reinforced by recurring back problems that kept me off the basketball court, distancing me from my former teammates. So when Beatríz found me drinking alone at La Fragua one night, I was glad for the company.

She glided in wearing a flowing flowered skirt, spied me at one of the low tables in the bar, and approached. On virtually all occasions, in those days, women of all classes wore dresses or skirts, as did all schoolgirls, since uniforms were universally required in government schools. It made Mexican women seem more feminine and proper to me than blue-jean-clad American women, more womanly and formidable. And like most mejicanas who walked the hilly, cobbled streets of San Miguel de Allende, often in high-heeled shoes, Beatríz moved gracefully on shapely tan legs, the skirt enhancing the image of fluidity and the mystery of movement, suggesting a lithe sensuality. She stood over me and asked:

"¿Me recuerdas?"

"Sí, sí. Of course I remember you. Please join me. But I've forgotten your name."

Even after she told me, I didn't recall ever knowing it. She was a friend of Licha and had worked as a barmaid at one of the clubs where Licha and I drank and danced. I don't know if I had ever spoken to her other than to say "hola" or "adiós."

She asked: "Have you talked to Licha?"

I nodded. "After the earthquake in De Efe I called to see if everything was okay with her and her family."

Beatríz pursed her lips. She was not unattractive, though without Licha's stature and presence. More petite, more Indian. I offered her a cigarette. We sat smoking while she filled me in on news of mutual friends. Then she asked how my writing was going.

I guess Licha must have told her that I was constantly scribbling away in my journal and writing stories, for in those days I hardly ever confessed to being a writer. In my eyes, despite the thousands of manuscript pages I'd penned, I wasn't a writer because I hadn't published any of my fiction. Whenever someone learned I was writing and asked how it was going, I changed the subject as quickly as possible, for it was a touchy subject with me. What does an unpublished writer say? Mexicans were the worst to let know you were a writer. The first thing they'd ask, ingenuously, was, "Where is your book? I want to read it now."

On one level I was a published writer, for I'd been working as a journalist, corporate hack, and freelancer since I was twenty-five. But I was embarrassed by my commercial writing, my "hooring," as Schifrin called it. So with Americans, who had the annoying habit of asking "What do you do?" as soon as they knew your name, I developed a litany of evasions: "What do you need done?" Or, "I play basketball," which was not untrue if not responsive to the implicit question. Or, "This and that," which made me mysterious, I thought.

But I had no reason to be evasive with Beatríz. She apparently knew something of my travail as a writer from Licha and seemed genuinely interested in my work. At the time I was reworking an early draft of *Flesh*, which ultimately would be my first published novel and about which I was hopeful. So I told her a bit about the story of Nick Petrov and his search for his father's bones in the fictional Mexican town of Escondido.

For some reason, as I spun the story out, she seemed fascinated by it, bringing her fingers to her mouth, staring at me, hanging on my every word. When I finished my rambling summary, she asked, "Did he ever learn how his father died?"

I shook my head. "He would never be certain."

She seemed to gaze at something inside herself. "Yes. Death is a mystery."

She pointed toward my pack of Faros lying on the table. "¿Se puede…?"

I held it out to her. "Por favor."

After I lit her cigarette she blew out a stream of smoke, leaned across the low table, and whispered:

"Last week I discovered the corpse of my fiancé."

The waiter came by, and I ordered a tequila for her and another beer for myself. She continued:

"I had not seen Homero for three days. I went to his house, but it was locked. Then I called his father in San Luis Potosí. He came to San Miguel and together we returned to Homero's casita. Again we knocked but again there came no answer. His father got a tool from his car to pry open the door, and we gasped at what we saw.

"All the sculptures and pottery Homero had created had been smashed on the floor. Likewise in the kitchen, where all the dishes lay broken underfoot. The whole house had been vandalized, but Homero was not to be found.

"His father said, 'My son must be on a borrachera to

have done this to his own work. When he sobers up he'll come back. We should clean the house for his return.'"

Beatríz chewed her bottom lip, sipped her tequila, and took a compulsive puff on her cigarette. With her fingers she combed back the straight, black hair that had fallen across her square-jawed face.

"I went to the bathroom, where the tub sat full of white water with towels floating in it. Beside the tub lay an empty sack of lime, which Homero used to make his plaster. This, I saw, is what had made the water white.

"I knelt beside the bath and began to pull the towels from it. Pero, con los toallas vino piel, piel blanco..."

Her eyes had glassed over. She looked at me, but I could tell she did not see me but rather the thing she described. However, I was not certain what she meant. With the towels, she had said, came "piel blanco," white leather or white skin.

"...piel, piel, mas piel..."

She made grasping motions with her hands, pulling motions with her arms.

"...skin, skin, more skin. It covered my arms and lay on the white water. I must have called out. Next I remember Homero's father pulling me away."

She threw back the rest of her tequila and lit another Faro. Then she told me how the father had run his hand down the chain to pull the plug and how, as the white water drained, the shape of Homero's lime-eaten body rose through it.

We had another drink or two. Then I walked her home. When I left, she gave me the orange-and-blue cajita with the skeleton and his wheelbarrow.

*

The next afternoon, just after siesta, I was taking the sun in the patio, sitting in the sling chair and sipping at a cup of sweet black coffee. Migratory warblers flitted overhead. The fragrance of the limón tree behind me scented the air. I heard footsteps and turned.

Passing through Lupe's jungle toward his room in back strode the artist Weatherby, though, like many artists in San Miguel de Allende, he may have been primarily a bullshit-artist. I nodded a spare greeting and returned to my reading. But then his shadow fell across my book and lay immobile there. When I looked up he said:

"I understand you were with Beatríz last night."

I stared at him. Lanky, gaunt, and unshaven with scraggly blond hair, he looked like a time-traveler, perhaps a Led Zeppelin roadie somehow left behind a decade earlier. His slovenly aspect and an all-knowing air that I associated with journalists and English professors had put me off. This conversation didn't help.

I had always tenaciously guarded my privacy. I detested scrutiny and personal questions, giving misleading answers as deterrents. My obsession with privacy led me, in St. Louis, to live in a high-rise, where no one could look in the window and a doorman blocked free entry. It's why I often left my telephone unplugged until I needed to call out and why I had always preferred city life, where one could move about anonymously and disappear for months without anyone caring or even knowing.

But here in this Mexican pueblito stocked with curious gringos and bored mejicanos, a town in which one was funneled on foot down narrow walled streets and through the jardín, where all could witness one's comings and goings, a town that rumors winged across effortlessly like the boat-tailed grackles that migrated each evening to the jardín to pelt passersby with bird shit, here I felt like I'd been squeezed between two glass slides and slipped beneath a microscope.

"Yeah, I had a drink with her."

Weatherby raised his eyebrows dubiously but beneath my steady gaze did not question my assertion. But neither did he move on. He stood silently over me blocking the sun and interrupting my reading and tanning. I lowered my book and asked:

"Did you know her fiancé?"

He stroked his incipient mustache. "Ah, so you heard. A bloody awful thing. Yes, I knew Homero. Not much of a sculptor but not so bad as to merit getting coshed and drowned in his own bath. And the lime, now there was a grisly touch."

I nodded agreement. "She said the cops have no clue about who did it. Maybe some kids looking for money."

Weatherby pursed his lips. "Yes, that's her story."

"What are you saying?"

He fixed me with a meaningful gaze. "I'd be careful with that one, matey…" He looked over his shoulder as if checking for spies in the papaya tree behind him before turning back to me. "Some say she's the one who done him in."

I pictured Beatríz in my mind. She seemed so sweet, self-conscious, and vulnerable; so kind, considerate, and feminine; so Mexican. I shook my head.

"It doesn't seem possible."

"Well, you haven't seen her angry, have you? She's a jealous little bird, that one."

On that point, I took him at his word, which, along with his suspicions, was echoed by others in the following days. Ultimately I concluded that it might be best to let her grieve for Homero without my consolation. Soon I heard she left town. That happened a lot in San Miguel. People came, people went. Libertad completa.

But liberty, I was learning, did not mean escape from life's struggles. I saw that my own frequent comings and goings, to Mexico, Europe, and elsewhere, in fact comprised a search for home. I thought I had found, at least temporarily, a secure home in Lupe's garden. But learning of Beatriz's possibly homicidal passion made the walls of my hermitage seem less impregnable. In fact, death would soon penetrate them as well and come to spend the night with me.

X
The Vision

The day I found the dead woman began like most others: sipping coffee in Lupe's garden among the birds and plants, reading—that day Jung, who understood my search for wholeness—and making notes in my journal.

For breakfast I retrieved a ripe avocado that had fallen to earth during the night, cut it open, and picked a limón to squeeze onto it. Lupe ambled over to offer me a honeycomb that Chucha had brought from the campo. After a few hours I retreated inside to fix lunch, followed by an hour's siesta. Such was my contemplative life in those days.

As I was waking from my nap with a cup of gritty coffee, Chucha came scooting up the flagstones beneath the canopy of plants. Standing dappled by sun outside my door, she wrung her hands.

"¡Señor! ¡Señor Rico! Come! The señora needs your help."

At Lupe's kitchen table sat a gringo I'd seen about town recently, usually well oiled. Head in hands, he mumbled incoherently. Lupe, who hovered over him, explained that this was the husband—estranged, presumably—of the blonde woman who had recently rented the upstairs apartment. He had a problem that Lupe could not grasp, and she asked me to translate.

"What's wrong?" I said to him in English.

He looked up to me and whined: "I haven't seen her for three days. We were supposed to meet last night but she didn't show. Now she's not answering her door. My God! I'm afraid something's happened."

I looked at Lupe, who stood rigid and wide-eyed, and paraphrased his concerns to her in Spanish. She crossed her arms over her chest as if cold. Neither had she nor Chucha seen the gringa for days. I turned back to the husband.

"Did you try the door?"

"It's locked." His voice cracked. "Something bad has happened. I just know it."

I smelled whiskey on him. Gaunt and unshaven, maybe fifty, he looked as if he'd slept in his clothes. Later I learned he'd been a state senator in Oklahoma.

I asked Lupe, "Do you have the key?"

She took a key ring from Chucha and told her to stay with the husband.

Out in the passageway that fed off the garden, afternoon sun warmed the white walls. I knocked on the thick wooden door and put an ear to it. Then I shook my head. Lupe stood mute, tensed, leaning on her cane.

I unlocked the bottom latch and pressed on the door. Nothing. Then the top bolt. The door swung open. I leaned inside and called, "Hello! Hello…" I turned to Lupe. "¿Su nombre?"

"Miriam."

"Hello, Miriam? Are you home?"

Lupe had introduced us when she first moved in. A not-unattractive woman of perhaps forty, full-figured. We'd passed in the garden a couple times. She smiled, but we did not speak. Maybe she wanted to talk, but I was too preoccupied with my own musings.

I motioned to Lupe to wait downstairs and mounted the stone steps traveling up to the apartment. I'd never been in the apartment before, which Lupe's daughter, Naomi, had occupied before recently moving to Querétaro to attend school.

The stairs ended at a small dining room with a dark wooden table covered by a white lace tablecloth. I moved down two steps to my left, toward the open door of a sunken bedroom and saw the blonde woman. She lay in white silk pajamas with her head thrown back, eyes open, mouth agape. Beside her on the bed lay a bulb-shaped inhaler that asthmatics used. Despite the warm afternoon sun pouring through the windows, her hand felt cold. Now I had to go downstairs and tell her husband.

Lupe sent me down the street to fetch a young, bearded doctor, a colleague of her son, who was a physician in Irapuato. I led him back to the house and up the stairs.

Despite my description of the dead woman, he took a step back and gasped when he saw the body. Maybe it was his first since med school.

"¡Muerta!" he uttered.

"De veras."

He held her wrist as if searching for a pulse, then shook his head. "Muerta."

Next he took a hand-mirror from his satchel, placed it to her face then examined it. "Está muerta."

Finally he unfolded a penknife from his pants pocket, jabbed the palm of her hand, and, getting no response, nodded. "Sí. Muerta."

Given her relative youth and the unexplained circumstances of her death, the police as well as the American consul would have to be notified and an autopsy performed, the doctor said. Lupe thought it best not to involve me, a foreigner, in any of this, planning to tell police that she had found the body and suggesting that I take a walk.

Just as well. I needed to get away from the house. Lupe and Chucha both appeared shaken by the woman's death, staring at me mutely as if looking for commiseration. But I shrugged it off. We all have to go when our time's up, I told myself. And in those days I was fool enough not to knock on wood or say a prayer to keep Death well away from me.

*

That evening a northerly wind rose up, and the air suddenly came hard and cold. "Un mal viento de Tejas"—a bad wind from Texas—I joked with Lupe, who believed that most of Mexico's problems originated in *El Norte*. But she did not laugh.

Feeling unusually restless, I strolled down toward the jardín. But what with the weather, few people were on the street and the town square lay deserted. I looked inside La Fragua hoping to find my friend Patrick Mulcahy, but the place was dead, and I saw no one I knew other than the *mesero*. After drinking a tequila I headed back to my room and the Simenon mystery I'd started the night before.

In my fireplace I built a blaze of mesquite sticks I'd bought from an old campesino who came to town with the wood tied to his burro, kindling it with kerosene that Lupe had provided. From the mantel I took the Oredáin bottle, poured two inches of amber tequila into a thick glass, and settled back in bed with my book.

The wind rattled the wooden shutters and the ill-fitting door, secured with an eyehook. Falling avocados drummed the roof. Then a spark shot from the fireplace with a crack, and I looked up. There, at the rustic desk, arm draped over the back of the black, Spanish armchair, sat the dead woman, leering at me.

I passed my hand over my eyes, and she went away. I let out a breath. What would Dr. Jung say—a projection from my unconscious? Perhaps finding her dead that afternoon had affected me more than I admitted.

Or maybe I'd been reading too many murder mysteries at night, over-stimulating my imagination.

Or perhaps it was the tequila, a relative of mescaline, making me hallucinate.

Or maybe it was just Mexico. Death was everywhere: stiffening burros in ditches, pine coffins stacked four-high inside shops you passed on the street, daily funeral processions to the Panteón, sugar-sculpture skeletons for sale at the market. The Mexicans seemed obsessed with death, which rubbed off on you.

Or maybe it was a ghost. But I knew there were no such things as ghosts, no credible scientific evidence for their existence. So I went back to my book.

Still, after a minute I could not help glancing toward the desk, and there she sat with her mocking gaze. "What do you want?" I blurted, and she disappeared.

After a couple more tequilas I managed to get to sleep, but left the light on all night and did not sleep well.

*

Next morning when Lupe limped into the patio, I told her about my vision of the dead woman, and her jaw dropped. She waved her hands in a distancing gesture, not wanting to encourage or participate in such talk, then shivered histrionically as if indicating fear. But she did not question that I had seen Miriam.

To the contrary, the following morning when we met, Lupe immediately asked, "Has she gone?"

I shook my head. "Ya no." Not yet.

For Miriam had returned a second night to the black-painted armchair, ashen-faced, fixing me with an aggressive, sluttish gaze. It was as if she was challenging me to seduce her in death after ignoring her while alive. Again I had not slept so well.

The wind blew for three days. For three nights Miriam haunted me. I slept with the light on for fear that, in the dark, she might somehow molest or harm me. Lupe avoided the garden, staying inside the kitchen of her casa, leaded-glass doors shut tight, and averting her eyes whenever I passed. Chucha was nowhere to be seen.

I cannot explain this haunting, why she chose to visit me or what she wanted. As Lupe later admonished me when I looked for an explanation, "Only gringos seek reasons for things supernatural. Why did the Virgin present herself to Juan Diego at Tepeyacac? Who knows? One cannot ask why. They are mysteries."

Nor can I explain why the haunting ended. But on the fourth day, the fierce wind from the north disappeared, and the air once again hung warm and calm. That night Miriam, too, vanished and never returned.

XI
Dark Souls

Though my sojourns to Mexico helped redeem me, they were hardly seamless idylls. One my most depressing days, I recall, came at Thanksgiving. Of course it's solely an American holiday, which Mexicans, except those catering to Americans, rightly ignore. I had agreed, halfheartedly, to meet Hal Bennett and Trevor Dennis for an afternoon Thanksgiving comida. I had mixed feelings about it because I had mixed feelings about both men. But I had nothing better going on.

At times Hal could be the best of companions: humorous, insightful, full of good cheer and camaraderie. As a fellow writer who had had some early success as a novelist and short-story writer—according to his accounts, he'd once been pegged as the next James Baldwin, the new black literary hope—he was supportive of my struggle to learn my craft, and suggested new approaches. We'd talk not only of literature and writing but also of politics, Mexican culture, women, art, and more, always with a sense of writerly investigation. We'd also play Scrabble at The House of Wires, Hal's low-rent apartment with gerry-rigged electric lines running helter-skelter across the ceiling and down the ill-painted walls. We'd drink beer with cabbies, soldiers, Mexican neighbors, and occasional American pigeons, that is, gringos Hal was trying to pluck a few dollars from to help finance the writing of his next novel.

But at other times, when his psychotic self showed, I wanted to shoot him. Mean-spirited, paranoid, hallucinatory, and confrontational, he seemed a different man. In these moods he reveled in offending my "Caucasian propriety," as he sneeringly called it, by violating common standards of friendship and civility. When he got into one of these combative snits, I'd leave him to it. But this Thanksgiving Day I didn't realize it was on him until after I had found him and Trevor at the Cuban restaurant and sat down. I should have gotten up and left as soon as I saw his Mr. Hyde riding him. But I didn't, my Caucasian propriety again kicking in.

After we had ordered, he called the waitress over again and asked her to turn down the recorded music, a reasonable and appropriate request since it was loud enough to affect conversation. However, she soon returned saying that she was unable to do so because other customers preferred to listen. Hal gritted his teeth and talked through them menacingly.

"Mira, señorita. Look around you. Go on, look. Now tell me how many other customers are there? Yes, only four. Did you question those other customers as to their preference? No. So then don't come here and lie to me."

"Pero…pero Don Raimundo told me…"

"¡Chinga Don Raimundo!" Hal jumped up, gesturing wildly and switching to English: "Who is this lying motherfucker? I'll whip his ass."

The girl ran off in tears. Hal followed her to the kitchen to berate the proprietor, Don Raimundo, personally. I looked at Trevor and shook my head.

"A bit over the top, I'd say."

But, typically, he took Hal's side. "It's a racial thing, man. If we were white she would have turned the damn thing down."

"You want me to ask her?"

Trevor stared, not knowing what to make of my sarcasm.

Trevor Dennis was a black Jamaican who had lived for years in New York. An unhappy, self-conscious man who never knew his father, he grew up in terror of his emasculating mother and older sisters. As a young prison guard at Attica during the 1971 riots, he was taken hostage and apparently raped, though understandably he would not talk about it. Nor was his health good. He kept getting spiking fevers, accelerated heartbeat, and rashes, though doctors could find no cause. In retrospect I guess he had AIDS. But this was before much was known about the disease, particularly in Mexico. Finally he merely reiterated: "It's a racial thing."

"Well, it is now," I said, "the way Hal's behaving."

"That's bullshit. The bitch is a Cuban racist. I know the fucking Cubans. They're the worst. They smile and stab you in the back."

The volume of the music suddenly lowered. Soon Hal returned and slammed his chair against the stone floor before sitting.

"Fucking *Don* Raimundo. Pussy motherfucker."

"Racist bitch," Trevor repeated for Hal's benefit.

"Motherfuckers can't run a business," Hal put in. "The atmosphere and the music are for the pleasure of the customer, not the fucking help. If that fat fuck owner turns the music up again I'm going to kick his ass."

I had already ordered some Cuban chicken with fried plantain and felt trapped. I should have cut my losses, thrown some money on the table, and fled, but I stayed on. Eventually the conversation turned away from loud music and theories on restaurant management, but the rhetoric remained the same. Throughout dinner Hal and Trevor carped about racist conspiracies they perceived in most everything, feeding off one another's paranoia and touting revenge, murder, war, and black fascism.

I sat silent, thinking of home, of settling down to a Thanksgiving dinner with my mother and my dear friend Romana, saying a heartfelt and decorous prayer of thanks, and sharing our homemade meal, as we had done in previous years. I thought of pumpkin pie and TV football, of the high spirits and laughter. But instead of brightening my mood these reminiscences, when played against the ugly reality before me, pushed me into an even deeper funk.

However, Hal was right about one thing: My Caucasian propriety hampered me. I hadn't the will to walk away from this psychotic scene, forcing myself to sit through it, something I would never impose on another. Yet I did it to myself.

*

But no matter how dark my moods might swing, I encountered even darker souls along the way, at times frighteningly so.

Mexico can seem so beautiful and benign. You feel the bright sun falling warm on your skin. You smell the fragrant flowers. You see the smiling Indian women and their laughing children. Despite their hard lives, the people persevere with dignity and good humor. They seem so open and honest. You feel beneficent gods everywhere, life imbued with spirit. Thus, to the indolent visitor, Mexico comes to seem like an affordable Eden. But this is before proclaimed lifelong friends abandon you, merchants cheat you, lovers deceive you, and strangers rob you.

Yet even after you learn these wearying lessons you can still be seduced by Mexico's beauty and apparent peacefulness—at least as it was then, in the 1980s. And, an incurable romantic, you once again let your guard down. You wade off into an inviting blue sea oblivious to lethal undercurrents. I had seen it happen to others. Then it happened to me, though not without warnings.

One Sunday afternoon just before sunset I stopped by Hal's apartment and found him drinking beer with two uniformed soldiers, part of the drug-interdiction force stationed in an old nunnery near the center of town. Both had mostly Indian blood, seemingly. The thin one, Tomás, sat silent in his dark green fatigues, jaw moving laterally as if grinding teeth. The fat, talkative one, Carlos, had searing red eyes and a perpetual smile, a combination that made me immediately uncomfortable under his lazy but ceaseless gaze. He talked of the difficult life of the Mexican soldier:

"We are paid only fifty cents a day, with which we must feed ourselves." He looked to Tomás, who nodded confirmation. Carlos went on: "We are provided a cook and pool our money. But still it is impossible to live on that amount." I nodded too. "Claro. It is a crime."

Carlos leaned toward me. "¿Quieres comprar marijuana?"

I answered that I was not interested in buying any drugs. "I use only this." I held up my bottle of Victoria. He held up his, and the four of us clanked bottles together.

"¡Salud!"

Carlos leaned back in his chair and let out a sigh. "Qué dia. We have been hard at work since midnight. At a roadblock we snared a gringo…" He looked at me and apologized for the pejorative. "Perdón. We caught an American running drugs. But he would not cooperate. Time and again we ask, 'Where did you purchase the heroin? Who gave you the money to do so? Where were you taking it?' Three simple questions. But he chose not to cooperate."

From the corner of my eye I saw Tomás moving both his head and his jaw from side to side. Carlos continued:

"So we put him flat on the table and get the Tehuacán…" He paused to gesture with his beer, as if shaking a bottle of mineral water. "And tzip! Up the nose. We ask again: 'Where did you get it, who gave you the money, where would you deliver it?' But still no cooperation.

"So we turn him over on his stomach and pull up the shirt and…" Carlos slapped his palm on the arm of the wooden chair, the crack echoing sharp off the concrete walls and stone floor of the largely unfurnished room. "Con la pistola, flat, on the kidneys. Twice. And again. Once more we ask our three simple questions. But still no cooperation…"

Hal, who hunkered nearby on an inverted plastic seed-bucket, whispered in English from the side of his mouth: "You getting all this?"

I let out a breath and muttered beneath it: "Enough."

Carlos yawned and scratched his stomach where his shirt spread between buttons. "…Next we pull down his pants and get out the wire…" He went on to describe scorching his suspect's testicles with electricity from the wall socket.

Carlos sipped from his beer, gazed at me, and smiled. The sun was setting, the room growing dark. I returned his smile, finished my beer, and left as soon as seemed polite.

*

A week later I arrived at Hal's place just as Carlos was leaving. Still on duty, he had stopped by to mooch a beer, a luxury that he himself could not afford. As he exited he let his eyes rest on me a moment, then pulled the door closed behind him. I shivered and turned to Hal.

"That guy gives me the creeps. Why does he keep looking at me like that?"

Hal lifted his chin and slapped my biceps with the back of his hand. "He wants to fuck you, man."

But Carlos was far from my mind as late one night I sat drinking a beer at a fruit stand in a small plaza on the lower side of town, a simple place that served fresh juice, cold beer, and sandwiches of jalapeño, goat cheese, nopal, and salty ham to neighborhood Mexicans. Occasionally I ate lunch there, for the woman who ran it always wore a starched dress and a smile. Children who played in the plaza would join me at the counter in their navy-blue school uniforms and tell me of their studies.

Across the street sat a dusty cantina that I had been in but once, in broad daylight. The bartender had eyed me suspiciously and served me without speaking. The only other customer sat tapping a peso on his wooden table and staring at me. After one beer I left and never returned.

But on this warm and comforting night the cantina was not so quiet. Recorded ranchera music, plaintive Mexican country songs of love, nostalgia, and sorrow, most always with an accordion weeping in the background, floated over its warped café doors and across the street to where I sat with my beer. Mixed with the music I heard occasional shouts and laughter. Then voices rose. Next came the sound of breaking glass. The café doors burst open. A man stumbled through them backward, lurched across the flagstone sidewalk, and fell to his back in the dark, cobbled street.

The doors swung to and fro. Soon another man appeared there and paused. He eyed the man in the street and strode through the doors. I saw him silhouetted in the cantina light. Lanky. Trousers tucked into thick-soled boots. Hair cropped close beneath the flat-topped cap of the Mexican army. He stepped across the flagstones and into the street where the man lay, pausing over him hands-on-hips, bending at the waist as if to gauge his well being. Then he kicked his head.

Next he looked up and saw me sitting in the light of the fruit stand. His arms fell limp and hung ape-like at his sides. He stood frozen, regarding me coolly, as he had the man at his feet.

I too remained immobile, the beer on the counter cold and wet in my hand. The soldier took a step in my direction, and I raised the beer to my lips, watching. He weaved across the street toward me, and I felt the cold beer catch in my throat. He stepped up onto the curb, gesturing with his right hand for me to stand and approach. It was then that I recalled Carlos, Tomás, and the American prisoner with the scorched testicles.

I saw that it was neither Carlos nor Tomás but a seeming combination of the two: a man with Carlos' piercing red eyes and Tomás' thin build and grinding teeth. He wore the same green fatigues. As he neared I saw that blood dripped from his left hand, which had been slit open across the palm. I released my beer bottle, stood, and moved toward him as slowly as I reasonably could, trying to keep within the circle of light falling from the fruit stand and visible to the pleasant woman there, who for once had stopped smiling.

The soldier mouthed words, but his speech was so slurred by drink that I understood little. I shook my head and raised my arms in a gesture of incomprehension.

His eyes tightened. He barked: "¡Ven acá! Come here! Now!"

I'd lived in Mexico long enough and had heard enough stories of brutal injustice to understand that I was not in a facsimile United States. Here, under its Napoleonic Code, there was no Bill of Rights, habeas corpus, or presumption of innocence. One could sit in a Mexican jail days or even years without charges or trial for alleged infractions. I had also heard stories of drugs being planted on suspects and ex-onerating evidence and witnesses disappearing. And of San Miguel de Allende police department reluctance to investigate the murder of a "pinche gringo," in the words of one officer called to a homicide scene. Despite a pretense of democracy, Mexico remained a police state where a campesino or tourist—say, myself—could disappear without any official notice or interest.

Realizing that, I now made a decision neither to comprehend nor speak Spanish. I reasoned that the more I acted like a vacationing gringo, that is, someone accustomed to civil rights, ambassadorial intercession, and the power of the United States government behind him, the less likely I was to be treated like a Mexican, that is, like a disposable someone without rights. Again I shook my head.

"I don't understand. No hablo español. English? Do you speak English?"

He stepped to me, into the circle of light, staggering, muttering. Then he reached for me.

I stood stone still as he ran his hands down me, searching. For what? A weapon? Drugs? I stared at the woman behind the counter of the fruit stand, whose eyes riveted on mine. I sensed blood pulsing through my temples; my ears rang. A palpable fear rose in my chest—a bitter taste of bile—with the realization of my vulnerability. If for whatever reason this man wanted to take me to the interrogation room in the old nunnery where the electric wire and mineral water awaited, there was no authority to stop him. If he wanted to share me with Carlos and the rest of the soldiers, it was his party. At least so I thought at the moment.

In retrospect I realize that was unlikely, given the scrutiny of most everything public or private in the small town. But that was not my reasoning at the moment. I felt a singular terror and powerlessness—a daily fact of life for many Third World people. And one question lodged in my mind: What should I do if he wants to take me with him?

As he was drunk and seemingly unarmed, I could likely break free and outrun him, assuming he had no pistol under his tunic.

Or I could stay put and play stupid, understanding no Spanish and passively resisting, in hopes that the fruit-stand woman would summon the police if things turned ugly. But whose side would they be on? Further, that strategy could buy me a head-kicking on the spot. I might be carted away unconscious and drugs planted on me.

Or I could cooperate and do whatever he asked, trusting that I would not be misused. I had broken no law. Cooperate: That's what fat, red-eyed, lusting Carlos had suggested in his Parable of the Uncooperative Gringo.

But after a moment, unable to communicate with me and under the steady stare of the fruit-stand proprietor, the soldier seemed to lose interest and merely staggered away.

I looked to the woman, whose gaze now lowered. I followed her eyes and saw my blue work-shirt and off-white jeans streaked with brilliant red blood.

*

Perhaps at last I had gained too much knowledge about my former Eden. Where once I felt secure in San Miguel de Allende, I now sensed a spirit of danger in the night air, both on the streets and in the bars. The incident with the drunken soldier breached in me a dam of denial about numerous unsettling occurrences in and around the town: shootings, knifings, muggings, rapes, fatal car wrecks, freak accidents, infectious diseases, capricious cops, violent soldiers, bad luck, and perverse fate. Mexico exhibited little justice of any sort—criminal, vigilante, or divine—with the possible exception of an ironic variety that came when least expected and with devastating results. It was no wonder Mexican men saw death as a joke. For a time I, too, had viewed the danger all about me with dark humor. I liked to repeat my Irish friend Patrick Mulcahy's admonition when things got, as usual, fucked up: "Remember, lads," he'd say in his brogue, "it's t'e T'ird World."

But then another incident, a shooting at The Ring *discoteca*, where I had danced with Licha, spooked me even further. A man from Guerrero, somehow insulted, pulled a gun and fired three shots, killing two young men and wounding a third. One of the dead, celebrating his upcoming wedding, was the nephew of Hal Bennett's landlord, who was evicting Hal to make room for the newlyweds. With too much to drink during his protracted bachelor party, the nephew had passed out at his table. A stray bullet entered his neck, and he never knew what hit him. The wedding was off, of course, and Hal didn't have to move after all. The shooter, it turned out, was a bodyguard for the governor of Guerrero and released into the governor's custody, i.e., set free thanks to his political connections.

But this was just one of a string of violent episodes—so many for such a small town—that were making me chary about staying in San Miguel: This, The Ring shooting. The murder of Beatriz's boyfriend. The strangulation and burial in a shallow campo grave of Ronald, the homosexual lover of American tennis coach Carlos, who was arrested for it. The killing of the singer Teodoro, who had been bound, beaten, and left to die in his home by presumed burglars. The taxi driver Jorge who disappeared, only to be found weeks later hanging from a tree in the hills near Guanajuato, having been robbed and raped. Further, there was the mugging of my friend Novedades and the knifing of a wealthy gringo who lived on the hill. The latter, however, came after some apparent provocation. The victim had called a cabbie a "fucking greaser" for overcharging him, figuring he couldn't speak English. But the taxi driver was sufficiently bilingual to get the gist and stuck a blade in the gringo's stomach. The American was shipped to a hospital in the States to mend, and the cabbie, after spending two weeks in jail, went back to work. Additionally, Alfonso, a friend and co-worker of Licha, was killed with two compadres in a car wreck. Other San Miguel residents committed suicide. Some got hepatitis or amoebas and wasted away. Some overdosed on drugs.

I probably underestimated the role drugs played in luring many Americans to Mexico, though I knew of those using pot, pills, cocaine, mushrooms, and other substances. But I avoided most Americans and particularly those who seemed damaged, a considerable number. I saw why Mexicans there held a low opinion of gringos. Too many Americans who came were not the polite, quiet, and relatively sober Midwesterners I knew. Rather, San Miguel drew flocks of snowbirds with broken wings: drug addicts, psychotics, family retainers, ex-cons, drunken misfits, embittered has-beens, and overbearing egotists. You would see the worst cases wandering about town in a disheveled daze, dancing crazily in the jardín to some internal music, braying English in the restaurants, or hooting drunkenly in the bars.

One such lost soul was Martina's new boyfriend, Morris. As a young man he had been a cantor in Brooklyn, he once told me, then a successful jazz drummer who recorded with top artists, then a heroin addict who fled to Mexico and lived for years in Pacific-coast beach towns, sleeping in hammocks under *palapas* or on the sand. But he had successfully straightened himself out, at least for a while. Unfortunately, I knew nothing of his dark background when I'd introduced him to Martina.

He then soon began to slide into alcoholism. The last time I saw him I was breakfasting at the Mesón del Matador. He sat sipping a beer while a Mexican amigo listened, shaking his head as Morris told him of his rough morning.

"I don't know what got into me," I overheard him say, "but I took that .357, loaded it and fired." He dropped his head to the tablecloth. "Can you beat that? Shooting my own damn car."

They came from the West Coast as well. Like the young man Adam Woolf, who, with his Valley friends, had been a doper since age ten. Together they had passed twenty years sitting in his parents' garage getting high and listening to music, all funded by their drug sales to youngsters. Like me he was in Mexico searching for the better parts of himself.

The danger and dysfunction of the town contrasted against an orderly and traditional Mexico that I enjoyed at my residence and was embodied in Lupe and her husband, Gerónimo. His reassuring, fatherly presence further induced me to remain within the walls of my garden. For he moved in a stoic world of propriety, sobriety, and taciturn discipline that suggested a Mexico before mass media, pop culture and narcotraficantes, that is, before its Americanization. Gerónimo's stony demeanor and censorious gaze at times unnerved my guests if he happened to greet them at the main door that opened onto the street.

"Who is that spooky motherfucker?" Hal once said, bursting into my room. "He looked at me like I'd stolen from the collection plate." I'd never seen Hal, usually so arrogant and commanding, so obviously cowed.

Gerónimo's stern look was that of a grade-school principal, a job from which he had but recently retired. Lupe's second husband, he was as handsome as she was homely. With silver hair always neatly brushed, a lank, olive-skinned face, square shoulders, and spare movements, he resembled the old film actor César Romero. He always wore creased dress slacks (light gray, usually) and a pleated guayabera (white or pale blue). Though he seldom spoke, his proud bearing and steely stare commanded respect, or intimidated.

Adriana, who soon was to enter my life like a guardian angel and guide me out of my darkness and solitude, was one of the few at whom he ever smiled. One day as I sat reading in the back of the patio, I heard the doorbell and rose to answer it, as I was expecting her. But as I got halfway across the garden, I saw Gerónimo and Adriana in the fern-lined passage from the street, he bowing economically and she curtseying floridly, spreading her flowing skirt with her hands and touching her brow to her knee, like a *duquesa* before a grandee. Then, as she moved toward me, hips swaying beneath the silky skirt, I saw a smile pass momentarily across Gerónimo's mustached lips as his eyes followed her.

He acted the role of Spanish *don* as well with Lupe's daughter, Naomi, who claimed that Gerónimo treated her with a protective love, as if she had been his own daughter. She attended college in Querétaro, boarding with a local family and traveling by bus back to San Miguel de Allende on weekends. Each Sunday evening when it came time for her to return to Querétaro, Gerónimo would walk Naomi to the bus station, buy two tickets, and ride the thirty miles with her. He'd then escort her to her door and ring the bell. When the dueña answered, he would say simply, "Here is my daughter." And with that, he entrusted Naomi to her weekday chaperones, returning on the next bus to San Miguel, his duty satisfied.

Each day just before noon Gerónimo would take a walk. Sometimes I'd see him in the jardín but always alone, as if his years as school principal and his hard gaze kept other sanmiguelenses at bay. Whenever we met there he'd give me a near-imperceptive nod and say merely, "Buenos," as if "Buenos días" was too chatty.

But he was always correct, if watchful, with me. Over the years he came to accept me as someone who might be trusted despite my being a gringo, that is, someone outside the sphere of custom and courtesy in which he lived. Or maybe it was just that after Naomi had married and moved away he could relax his guard against Americans, i.e., known fornicators.

At times we exchanged a few words when we met in the patio, usually about the weather or some proximate event. But he was always quietly helpful when I needed aid, meticulously tying with twine a basket I was shipping north and building a small desk, from scrap lumber, that I needed for my work. He presented it to me with the words, "Es bien rústico."

That describes Gerónimo as well: rustic. Made of strong material, staunch and without ostentation. He is gone now,

I recently learned. With his passing a window to old Mexico closed, a Mexico of strict manners and self-discipline, of quiet courtesy and responsibility. A Mexico that looked upon the increasingly Americanized world with a knowing and disapproving gaze.

XII
The Rabbit Man's Surmise

I knew I'd been spending a lot of time alone. But I didn't realize how much until Ernesto alerted me to what lay behind the rabbit man's persistence.

Time and again as I was sitting alone at La Fragua, a café, or restaurant, the rabbit man would appear in the doorway, survey the customers, and make a beeline to me. Dressed in traditional white, campesino homespuns that he also sold, he approached with his cloth sack on his left shoulder and on his right hand a white, fake-fur rabbit. He'd stand over me, look down with a questioning expression, and work the hand puppet.

"¿Conejo?" he would ask. "Rabbit?"

I'd shake my head and go back to my tequila, to my meal, to my solitude.

I had a lot of solitude then. Certainly traipsing off to Mexico, leaving behind kith and kin, and secluding my-self in the walled garden of Lupe's casa suggested a certain monkish impulse. As did, in a way, my attending Sunday Mass at La Parroquia, the fanciful pastel-pink parish church designed by an illiterate mason who drew its plans in the sand. It resembled more than anything else the Disney Fantasyland castle. That, and the perceived childishness of visiting gringos, led mejicanos from the more serious surrounding towns of Dolores Hidalgo, Irapuato, and Celaya to refer to San Miguel de Allende as "San Mickey Mouse."

I never told anyone that I went to Mass. I wasn't even Catholic and had been a proclaimed atheist and spiritual skeptic ever since I started reading assorted behaviorists in college. Humankind was a blank slate, I'd learned. All is nurture. Nature and what lay inside, including any dubious spiritual essence, held no necessary sway over us. That's what I had been taught. But now I was having doubts. I'd sit at the back of the dim, candlelit church among weathered campesinos clutching straw hats and Indian women nursing infants wrapped in their rebozos. The white-frocked priest went on in Spanish, which I tuned out, staying with my own homegrown meditations. This solemn sanctuary seemed a good, cool spot to be alone with myself despite the encircling throngs of silent people smelling of wood smoke, perspiration, and dust.

Further meditation came in my garden sanctuary, where I slid in and out of my reading, lapsing into musings, self-examinations, and journal entries stimulated by Conrad, Katherine Anne Porter, Turgenev, and Orwell; by

Jung, Lawrence, and Freud; by Henry Miller and Hemingway. Porter's short story collection *Flowering Judas*, which Arnold Schifrin had recommended, sent me off on long deliberations on the tragic beauty of Mexican life; Turgenev's *Fathers and Sons* took me back to the cathartic death of my father seven years earlier, which still haunted me; Jung's theories on the unconscious speaking through dreams made me ponder my own; Hemingway, the existential moralist, made me wonder about courage and how a man might best carry himself in a seemingly indifferent and hostile world.

He also reminded me of my own self-destructiveness, though it was rather tame compared to that of Hemingway, whose booze-filled, accident-prone, and ultimately suicidal later years set the self-destruction bar far too high for the likes of me to hurdle. Nor did my self-destructive tendencies match those of some drinkers and druggies who slid through town, or of the elderly women from New York, London, or Toronto who lived in big houses up in Atascadero and whom you read about in the *Sol del Bajío*, found dead of tranquilizer overdoses when the maid came Monday morning.

Nonetheless, in myself I saw a similar tendency in kind if not degree. Years of steady drinking. Not a quart of gin a day like Hem, but excessive and regular. Fifteen years of cigarettes and counting despite my nicotine-addicted father's heart attack and early death. Broken ankles, broken hands, stitched wounds, harrowing bike wrecks, and a taste for the dangerous demimonde of East St. Louis and De Efe. But its worst manifestation, potentially, came just months earlier, during my last lugubrious turn up north. I don't know what got into me. The full moon, maybe. Or the devil. It was as if I was really trying to kill myself.

I'd been in the city too long. I'd dealt with too many deadlines and demanding sons of bitches, picking up too much second-hand stress—much deadlier, I reasoned, than second-hand smoke. So I got the keys to a friend's river house for the weekend, a place near Nauvoo, Illinois, overlooking the Mississippi from high bluffs, three hours north of St. Louis.

But come Saturday night there, I grew restless and drove the ten miles to Keokuk, Iowa, to hit the bars. At a dive on Maine (sic) Street I met two gals headed up river twenty miles to a strip club at Fort Madison where their girlfriend worked. It sounded like a potentially interesting party, so I accepted their invitation.

I followed them up the black highway, the river lapping silver at its edge. We stopped at a gravel lot under the bridge on the Illinois side, at a blue metal shed. Inside the ill-lit, concrete-floor building, the sound of a rasping saxophone came from a jukebox in the corner. Farmers in bib overalls and tractor caps lurked in shadows along the walls. When an aging stripper plied a makeshift stage edged in fake-walnut paneling, only the bartender applauded. Soon, realizing I'd entered the most depressing joint in the free world, I left with a six-pack under my arm.

Beer bottle in hand I pushed my compact downriver, over a flat, two-lane highway running straight south across Illinois bottomland that flooded most every spring. I remember the full moon pouring through my windshield. It shone like platinum on the river, where deer came to drink. Though at this point, the upper Mississippi more resembled a lake than a free-flowing river, restrained by the hydroelectric dam at Keokuk, which sent power 150 miles south to St. Louis.

I smoked, I drank, I drove. I don't recall how many beers I'd had by then. Double-figures for sure. I held the pedal to the floor. The speedometer crept toward one hundred. I gave a passing thought to the possibility of a deer bounding across the roadway and through my windshield. At that speed, even hitting a possum could send me into the ditch and kill me. But I didn't care. It wasn't as if I was being chased or had anywhere to go. There was nothing behind me or in front of me. That's the way life felt then: I was racing alone down a dark highway.

But my self-destructiveness eased once I returned to Mexico. I began to live the life of a cleric: solitude, meditation, a glass or two of wine, chastity. I was turning inside, delving into my essence, whatever that proved to be. Except for but occasional company like Lupe or Ernesto, I kept my own counsel. I read. I meditated. I took long solitary walks in the campo. I dined alone. And when I did, the rabbit man would find me.

A square-shouldered, taciturn mestizo with cropped black hair, he'd always single me out, approach, and give me his one-word sales-pitch: "¿Conejo?" he'd ask, bobbing the toy rabbit, with its slender, fake-fur ears and button eyes, up and down.

At first I had responded with a simple, "No, gracias." But after the third or fourth time he had approached me over a period of weeks, I told him: "No. No, gracias. No tengo niños. And since I don't have any children, I don't need a puppet."

But he simply shrugged, worked the bunny some more, and reiterated, "¿Conejo?"

A week later I dined alone at El Mesón del Matador, a small, inexpensive grill with wrought-iron-and-glass doors, run by a stooped ex-bullfighter. His head always hung to the side, as if the picador's lance had severed his neck muscles as well as the bull's. The food and décor—including torturous straight-backed chairs—did not much recommend the restaurant. But I returned many times, perhaps because of the lighthearted Mexican ambience and smiling staff. The owner set the tone by imprinting on the back of the menu: "If our food pleases you, please return. If not, recommend us to your friends. They will enjoy the joke."

However, that appealing air was being disturbed that evening by a loud Texan, seemingly, who demanded in English immediate attention and fast service. He questioned the cleanliness of the kitchen and refused to drink the filtered water served him.

"Now cook that hamburger well done," he bellowed. "¿Entiende? No sangre. Well done. Bien hecho. Understand?"

The waiter, a handsome young man in his twenties, nodded courteously. I sat avoiding eye contact with the Texan, trying to appear as Mexican as I could, chatting with the waiter in Spanish and reading that morning's *Excelsior*, which someone had left behind. My sympathies were with the waiter, and I did not want to get drawn into conversation with my nominal countryman as if I was his ally.

Finally, the waiter brought him his platter and returned to the kitchen. The Texan grabbed the catsup bottle and lifted the top of his bun.

"Hey, you! Come back here. There's no hamburger. Where's my hamburger?"

After a moment the waiter sauntered out from the kitchen and gave the Texan a servile bow. "Sí, señor. Para servirle."

"There ain't no hamburger in this bun."

The waiter peered at the plate as if puzzled.

"¿No hay hamburgesa?"

"No. That's what I'm saying. You didn't give me any meat."

"No es posible. ¿Dónde está?" said the waiter, bending to glance beneath the table as if searching there for the missing hamburger.

I heard muffled laughter coming from the women in the kitchen as the Texan turned catsup-colored. Again bowing, the waiter retrieved his plate. "I will look in the kitchen. Perhaps it is there." I held my newspaper up, smiling behind it as the waiter passed with a wink.

The incident typified for me Mexicans' obliqueness, tolerance, and humor. Rather than confront the Texan and try to correct his rudeness, as I likely would have done in his shoes, the waiter simply accepted his customer as a congenital asshole and wrung some sly fun from the situation.

After the Texan had wolfed down his food, paid, and retreated, my dinner arrived. As I bent over my grilled goat I heard the metal door to the sidewalk scrape across the stone floor and looked up. In the doorway stood the white-clad rabbit man, a furry puppet on his hand. Its front feet waved a greeting. Approaching, he asked:

"¿Conejo?"

"Remember me? I told you I don't have any children."

He tilted his head, glanced to the puppet, then, with raised eyebrows, gazed back at me. "¿No quieres conejo?"

I laid down my fork. "Look. You're wasting your time with me. I don't need a puppet. I don't have children and probably never will. I don't want a fucking rabbit."

"Are you sure?"

I lowered my head as if the picador's lance had pierced me as well and moved it back and forth. Fucking Mexicans.

Having finished eating, I walked down the hill to La Cucaracha. After the episode with the rabbit man I needed a drink. There, as I walked through the cantina's doorway, I found Ernesto leaning glassy-eyed on the bar.

I supposed that Ernesto was somewhere in his fifties, but with shining black hair, black mustache, and the energy of a man half his age. He wanted me to write his life's story, which had begun in Texas with his birth to migratory Mexican farm workers. Ernesto's mother, jealous of his father's first wife, who had died giving birth to her ninth infant, demanded parity. Ernesto was the result: his family's eighteenth and final child. Raised in Mexico, Ernesto, when threatened with induction into the Mexican Army at age seventeen, fled to the U.S., where he was also a citizen thanks to his Texas nativity. Within months he was drafted into the U.S. Army, trained as a sniper, and sent to Korea.

"I couldn't even speak English," he once told me. "I didn't know if I was Mexican, American, Korean, or Chinese, so I just shot everything that moved, red, yellow, white, black, whatever their color."

But now, despite having spent time in U.S. jails for running wetbacks across the Rio Grande, he was a successful businessman with a family, a small factory of artisans, and a superabundance of true tales and camaraderie. He bought me a beer, and we toasted our good luck, that of being Americans who got to live in Mexico instead of, say, Detroit. He lowered his bottle and asked:

"Where have you been, amigo?"

Such was the state of my cloistering. I was avoiding even Ernesto, or at least the haunts where we usually met up. I shrugged.

"Haven't been drinking much."

He frowned and laid his hand on my shoulder. "You sick or something?"

I smiled. Vintage Ernesto. He lived life wide open, at a hundred miles an hour. Anything less in anyone else, particularly a drinking buddy, was a puzzling cause for concern.

"No. Just keeping to myself, I guess. Doing some thinking."

"I don't like that thinking business, Rick. Gets you in trouble. Let yourself go. The world will take care of you, one way or another."

Then a flash of white behind Ernesto drew my eyes to the sidewalk beyond the cantina's doors, where the rabbit man passed with his wares. Luckily he'd not seen me. I lifted my chin toward the doorway.

"You know that cabrón with those damn conejos?"

"Miguel? Sure."

"The pendejo won't leave me in peace. Whenever he sees me sitting alone, he tries to sell me one of his rabbits. I've told him a hundred times I don't have any kids. I don't know why he thinks I'd need a fucking *conejo*."

Ernesto spit a mouthful of beer across the bar. He doubled over, coughing and gagging. When he came up, a wide grin stretched across his dark red face and tears sat in his eyes. He put his arm around me in a *medio abrazo*.

"You silly sonofabitch. 'Conejo' is like 'pussy' in English. Those rabbits aren't for kids. They're for lonely gringos like you to jerk off with. Miguel makes a killing with them."

I stared at Ernesto. "Are you serious?"

My incredulity convulsed him once again. Between guffaws he called to the bartender. "¡Oye! ¡Jaime! Más cerveza. And two shots of Herradura. My lonely friend here needs to shake out the cobwebs."

I thought: Maybe Ernesto was right. If that's what people were thinking of me, maybe it was time to end my hermitage.

XIII
Letting Go

Friday evening, just days after learning of the service that Miguel, the rabbit man, provided the expatriate community, I sat in La Fragua nursing some clear tequila in a slender shot glass. Still alone, still unwilling or unable to make any effort in any direction to break from my self-imposed psychic imprisonment. Despite the sunshine and brilliant flowers, despite the daily drama of town life teeming all about me, everything seemed monochrome and uninteresting. And I didn't have the will to rouse myself out of my funk.

If I had wanted company, I could have gone to Mamma Mia's, usually crowded with tourists and ex-pats, or to an art opening I'd seen advertised. But I had no interest in tourists, not even pretty ones, and had been made wary of art openings. I'd gone to such San Miguel social affairs before, usually at some private gallery and usually out of courtesy to some artist I'd met. But I seldom stayed for more than one drink. Gringos whom you never saw in the markets, on the streets, or in the cantinas, would show up dressed as if for the country club. They seemed to know each other and talked loudly of bridge parties and of friends in New York. If they attempted to speak Spanish to a waiter, they did so ineptly. Some had come for the weather. Others had come to live in splendor up on the hill and lord it over servants, a lifestyle beyond their means back home. These sorts of people had, I felt, little to offer me.

Although at the time a couple thousand gringos lived among the fifty thousand Mexicans in San Miguel de Allende, I could pretty much avoid them if I wanted to, and most of time I wanted to. To me the Mexicans seemed more exotic and full of life than most *yanquis*, Brits, and Canadians. They had much to teach me about living, and I had much to learn. Further, I had spent my whole life among gringos and needed a break. I certainly didn't want to stand around an art gallery talking real estate and the cost of things, the two versions of the same topic, money, that dominated gringo conversation there.

I didn't give a fuck about money, a fact I had demonstrated only too well over the years. When I got some, I quickly managed to blow it, mismanage it, or give it away, as if in fear of contamination. The Mexicans reinforced my disregard for cash: the poorest and cheeriest folks I'd ever met. But that seemingly bothered other Americans in San Miguel de Allende. Time and again I'd heard them la-ment the poverty of the Mexicans. But these were often the same folks who, despite all their cash, credit, and real estate, seemed bored, depleted, and angry. I suspected that in their hearts they sensed that the ragged but smiling campesino on his burro was somehow better off than they were.

However, there were exceptions to my gringo-avoidance in San Miguel. I enjoyed the company of Peter Kosovic, a mad Czech-Canadian who liked to drink copious amounts of wine, play chess, and argue philosophy and literature; Bob Clelland, an ex-newsman who had covered Mexico City in the 'fifties, when they still drove cattle down the Reforma at night; Norman Popovsky, a yogi and long-time ex-pat with whom I shared East Side roots and who was always generous and kind; and Patrick Mulcahy, an Irish bookbinder transplanted to San Francisco, who sometimes blew into town with fine stories and solid camaraderie. But even these guys I didn't see often, choosing to be alone. However, tonight that sort of brooding gringo solitude was not to be permitted.

Arturo appeared in the doorway of the bar, spied me, and came over to shake hands. A lanky, handsome, and cheerful young artist, he painted haunting Mexican land-scapes in which a white river of campesinos dressed in tra-ditional homespuns marched ten-abreast into a setting sun. The landscapes changed, from the mountains, to the valleys, to the seaside, but the army of peasants continued to march silently, stoically, endlessly. His speech, too, was like a river, a stream that rushed by so fast that it was hard to get a paddle in.

"Hey, hombre, what are you doing sitting here alone, waiting for someone? If Mexican he probably won't show up so come with me to the Bellas Artes for an opening. My friend Elizondo is exhibiting and has bought some wine. Finish your tequila and let's go."

It was not a request but an order. I could not argue against such a strong will, as I then had little of my own. So I made my arguments for avoiding art openings silently, to myself, as we walked the cobbled streets together in the cool night. But when we arrived at the Bellas Artes I was relieved to find a largely Mexican crowd. They mingled under the portales, the covered archways that faced the central patio, their soft voices rising together in a soothing hum. A folding table had been arranged as a bar, where wine was being poured into plastic cups.

I got a cup of white wine. Arturo introduced me to Elizondo. Then I drifted under the portales to study his paintings. It was, as I recall, accomplished work. He had studied painting in Spain and the discipline showed. I thought of my own work. When would my discipline begin to bear fruit, if ever? Who would ever see my work? What would become of me? Questions every struggling writer asks. In the beginning you tell yourself you'll devote five years to it and see how it goes. Then ten years. After fifteen, you can't quit because it's part of you now, lodged irrevocably in your heart. But residing there with it is the fear that you will never be published, that when you die in some fly-blown garret your brother's children will come (since as a penurious writer you had neither the time nor the money for a family of your own) and throw your manuscripts in the dumpster. That ignoble end for your life's work is where all your striving will lead. That's the fear.

Then I looked up. Perhaps I had felt her eyes on me. Half-hidden behind a stone column stood a petite woman with wavy black hair cascading to her shoulders, perhaps twenty-five, maybe thirty years old. Dark eyelashes, high cheekbones and penetrating brown eyes; a soft, reddish glow to her light tan skin. Dressed in a black sweater and silky brown skirt, she was as beautiful as any woman I'd ever seen. She looked away and disappeared behind the column. I felt a hand on my elbow and turned to find Arturo beside me.

"Ven, amigo. There's someone here who wants to meet you."

He led me across the patio searching for whoever it was. He stopped by the makeshift bar, stood on tiptoes, and lifted his eyebrows. "Ah. There she is." And he led me to the black-haired woman in the flowing brown skirt, Adriana Márquez Lago.

"¿Conoces el pintor Elizondo?" I asked her.

"No, I know no one in town. Only my roommate, Claudia, who brought me here. And Arturo, whom I just met tonight. We moved to San Miguel de Allende last month from Puebla, with my daughter, Angélica."

I looked around. "Is she here?"

"No. Tonight she is with the maid."

Another woman with servants. Privileged, like Licha, and most likely spoiled, I thought. But I couldn't have been more wrong.

*

Adriana, Claudia and I walked together from the Bella Artes down the Salida de Dolores Hidalgo to the edge of town and turned up a dark, largely unpaved street, the Calzada de La Luz. Plain, two-story homes lined one side of the street, gerry-rigged hovels the other. As we passed a low home of irregular stones with a roof of commandeered road signs, a mongrel rushed from the dark to growl and snap at us. Adriana bent as if to pick a stone from the ground, and the dog scurried whimpering back into the night.

Under a bare, glaring bulb Claudia unlocked a thick wooden door and led us into a small apartment where the dining table sat by necessity in the middle of the living room. As a college-trained manager at the Atascadero, an old hotel half-way up the hill that guarded San Miguel de Allende on the east, Claudia was middle class. But here, unlike middle-class homes in El Norte, there was no television or VCR, no washer and dryer, no carpet, car, or garage. Being middle-class in Mexico meant you weren't poor; it meant you didn't live in hovel with a makeshift roof or in a dirt-floor, mud-brick home in the campo; it meant you didn't have to bend in the fields, haul sacks of concrete on your back all day, or beg in the streets.

For Claudia it meant working six days a week for a dollar an hour, sewing her own clothes, buying used furniture, and somehow making ends meet. It meant an itchy wool sofa with bad springs, a formica-topped dining table on a stone floor, and religious calendars as wall decorations. It meant washing laundry by hand on a concrete scrub-board in a shared patio and stringing it up to dry. But since this was Mexico, it also meant having a maid, who came with the rented apartment, to do it for you. The maid was not middle class and perhaps lived on the other side of the dark road in a home with a ceiling that read "Cuidado Con El Tren." And, since it was Mexico, Claudia's middle-class patio would have a fountain at its center ringed by scores of potted plants growing from carrot tins and plastic jugs beneath the dripping laundry: ferns, herbs, vines, and flowers: orchids, fuchsia and jasmine; lilies, roses, and geraniums; cilantro, sage, and thyme.

Adriana took an unopened bottle of tequila from the mantel and poured us each a shot.

"¡Salud!"

Claudia sat at the dining table. Adriana insisted I relax on the sofa and crossed her legs as she sat beside me. I said:

"You have a warm home. It reminds me of my grandmother's when I was a child."

Adriana flicked her hand dismissively. "Maybe because this is her sofa."

I asked them questions about their hometown. Soon we heard a soft knocking at the door. Claudia, who was as tall and substantial as Adriana was petite and lithe, strode to it in high heels on muscular legs. I did not know Puebla, but I figured it to be a mountain town like San Miguel, where women walked everywhere and sculpted their calves. She came back leading a fiftyish, silver-haired man whom I recognized, perhaps from La Fragua. I stood and shook hands. Mario was his name. He sat at the table but refused a tequila.

"I know your face," I said.

"I'm always about town. I run a building-supplies business, so I am everywhere."

He looked to Claudia. Claudia looked to Adriana. Adriana looked to me and said, "Come, let me show you my workshop."

She led me back out the front door and through a gate into the patio. There I followed her up a flight of metal stairs to a padlocked door.

"Mario seemed a little shy."

"Sí. Because he is married."

"Ah. But Claudia is an attractive young woman. Why Mario?"

"What else is there for a woman here? Not the guapos in the bars, who have all the gringas they want."

She took a key from beneath a flowerpot on the windowsill, unlocked the door, and led me inside a solitary room the size of mine on the Calle Margarito Ledesma. She flipped on a lamp over a wooden workbench.

"Here is where I make my jewelry, my mobiles, my sculptures."

She worked in brass, copper, tin, and steel wire, and with beads and seashells. Delicate mobiles dangled above her workbench, their shells washed about by minute waves of air.

On a folding card-table sat a hotplate and two dishes. Two cardboard boxes filled with children's clothing rested on the floor against the wall. In the corner lay a palm mat with two pillows. Adriana saw me focus there.

"This is also my home. That is where my daughter and I sleep. There is where I cook our meals. Here is where I work."

"Very efficient."

She laughed. "Sí. Somos muy eficientes. We waste neither time nor energy running from room to room. All is designed with efficiency in mind." She let her eyes wander about the room then gazed up at me. "Yes, it's a bit rustic. But it's all we need, Angélica and I. We are content."

I studied her. What a strange, exotic creature. What a life she had chosen for herself. Or perhaps Fate had chosen it for her. But I did not question her assertion of contentment. She stood barely five-foot tall and gaunt, but she stood solidly, calmly, contentedly. I nodded.

"I know people who live up the hill…" I lifted my chin

toward Atascadero. "…in grand homes with pianos and marble staircases who are not content."

"Claro. And tell me, Rick: Are you content?"

"At this moment, yes."

"What else is there but this moment?"

"Nada."

But I had lied. I was elsewhere—in the past, in the future, but not here and now. Living inside my mind instead of my body. I turned to go.

"You're not leaving?"

"Yes. I'm sorry. I'm tired." We shook hands. "Nos vemos pronto."

She nodded. "Yes. We'll see each other soon."

I moved back through the door, down the stairs, and out to the dim street. I walked away hands in pockets, stepping around potholes, questioning myself about my reclusive impulses, wondering where I belonged.

"¡Oye! ¡Oye!"

I stopped and turned. Adriana stood silhouetted beneath Claudia's porch light, motionless, arms at her sides. Then she slowly raised her arms halfway, in a gesture both of incomprehension and entreaty.

I stood stone still. I recalled Ernesto's words: "Let yourself go. The world will take care of you one way or another." And I felt his eyes on me.

So I did as he said: I lifted my arms as Adriana had done and walked back to her.

XIV
Life Is Trouble

Next day, a couple library books under my arm, I walked from my *apartamentito* through Lupe's garden and down the Calle de Correo. I stopped at the post office to check the *Lista de Correo*, the general delivery roll, but my name did not appear. I moved down the block past the mustached man who sold lottery tickets from his doorway, to the jardín. Under the portales I bid, "Buenos días," to the Indian woman cooking there from whom I sometimes bought a *gordita*. The aromas of frying chorizo, corn meal, and cilantro rose from her griddle. At the corner I bought a pack of cigarettes from the confectioner's wagon and crossed the Calle de San Francisco, where on the corner a man stood with a laden basket on the stones between his feet, calling "¡Espárragos! ¡Espárragos!"

I strolled past the Blue Door Bakery, waving to the cashier, Eduardo, an intense yet inept basketball player and former teammate. A block further on I turned at the pharmacy, veering past the indígena selling peanuts on the curb and moving toward the library. There I returned my Porter and Turgenev and checked out *Walden*, which I had not read for years. I longed for the solemnity of woods, clear waters, and green meadows, perhaps a projection of my dry, infertile psychological state. I longed for home.

With the paperback in my pocket I again made my way past the peanut woman, anticipating sitting in my sling chair reading Thoreau as warblers sang from the lime trees. But as I turned the corner I ran into Adriana, literally, as she stepped from the farmacia studying a packet of birth-control pills.

She stood on tiptoe and pressed a warm, fragrant cheek to mine. Then she shrugged dismissively at the packet in her hand. "No tienes obligación," she said.

Nonetheless, despite her reassuring disclaimer, I did feel obligated. A rational resistance to Adriana, though as impersonal as my previous irrational resistance, now rose to my consciousness. Getting involved with a woman, any woman, presents a dilemma. Perhaps partly from instinct and partly from experience, a man grows wary of making attachments too quickly. It's so easy and pleasant to establish a romantic relationship and all that it invokes. Often it takes no more than having sex but once. But dissolving that relationship, an eventuality in most cases, is seldom easy or pleasant. Further, getting involved is even worse in a small town like San Miguel de Allende, where your every act, even the most innocent, is scrutinized by someone, and rumors scurry about like rats, nibbling at your privacy and infecting your freedom.

Trouble. That's what you think: A woman means trouble. But as Ernesto told me, shrugging, after his wife learned of yet another mistress and banned him once again from their bedroom, "Life is trouble." And the one thing we must do, I was learning from my Mexican friends, is live life in the physical world, now.

So instead of returning home to spend the afternoon in New Hampshire with Thoreau, I took Adriana to comida in the patio of an old colonial home turned guesthouse, where she told me her life story, or at least part of it. But it was the part she left out and told me only later that explained so much.

*

Most moments in a life composed of moments are forever lost to us. Memory, thankfully, is selective, allowing us to discard the unimportant minutiae of daily life and retain those moments that, for better or worse, move us. Such was that afternoon with Adriana. Etched in my mind is a tableau that I can now peer at from a distance of years. In it Adriana and I sit at a wrought-iron table in the sunny patio of the Posada Carmina. Beside us water murmurs in a circular tiered fountain adorned with ferns and flowering vines. A greenish warbler sings from a jacaranda tree whose purple petals carpet the patio. The sun hangs high over

Adriana's shoulder in a blue sky with but one puffy cloud. The ambient air neither warms nor cools us. A half-emptied bottle of translucent wine rests on the white tablecloth that drapes toward the stone floor, brushing her brown paisley skirt and tan leg. She sits framed in a gracefully arched portal of the five-hundred-year-old casa, her shining black hair sharp against the whitewashed wall behind her. Her eyes glow moist from the wine; her face is flushed, her lips parted slightly as if to relish the liquor lingering on her tongue.

I am dark-haired and tanned, darker even than she where our bare forearms touch tangentially on the white linen. At this moment, as advised, I am living inside my body and in the present. I am tasting the wine, drinking in her beauty, sensing whispered wind and beneficent sun on my skin. I am savoring the warbler's song and the chiles in cream we have just eaten, aware of her soft patchouli scent carried to me on that slightest of breezes circling the courtyard. Her lilting provincial Spanish, for she speaks little English, floats across the table to me, and I nod at her revelation that she had deceived her husband on their wedding night—not with another man but into believing she was a virgin.

"He was so innocent. As was I. I had had but one lover. But the thought of that would have been too much for him to bear. So I tricked him."

"How?"

She purses her lips and blushes. Her eyes move from side to side. "Easily."

"Más tarde, si quieres, you can show me how you did it."

She stares at me, lips still parted, as if picturing it in her mind. She suppresses a smile. "I would do that if you wished."

I pour more wine. "I am trying to imagine how a young husband would feel about such things. I am trying to remember."

"It's easier to imagine if you are Mexican. For some men it is everything. In the capital some surgeons do only hymen reconstruction."

"And in the countryside there are no doctors."

She nods, thoughtful. "Sí. No hay médicos en el campo. Pero…"

"Tell me."

"Life there is hard but good." She takes a sip of wine. "As soon as I was able, I married and left home. Guillermo was no older than I and knew just as little of how to live. But we learned. We had a simple home on a hillside outside Puebla with candles for light and a fireplace for heat. For water there was a well and a bucket you lowered on a rope. Here, feel my arm…"

I reach across and wrap my hand around her biceps. It feels like a polished stone covered in kidskin. However, not until later, when she invites me to dinner, do I learn how soft she is at the core.

*

San Miguel was a small town made to feel even smaller

by houses built wall-to-wall, narrow streets, and the concentration of most everything one needed—library, bakery, market, church, bars, cafés, restaurants—within a few blocks of the jardín. Thus it was hard not to encounter friends and associates, particularly those you were trying to avoid. Most everyone walked everywhere and, unless you sneaked out to the market during siesta when others were sleeping, you bumped into them, as I had with Adriana.

Such serendipitous meetings multiply when synchronicity is in the air, when two people converge at precisely the right moment, when both, romantics to begin with, are vulnerable, melancholy, lonely, and imaginative. You keep on meeting again and again, at the library, the market, the café, the jardín. Then it is impossible, when the air is balmy, your day is free, her dark eyes are aglow, and her subtle perfume fills your head, at such synchronous moments it is impossible and foolish not to invite her back to your place for siesta. When it happens three or four times within a week or two, you shrug and give in. You have become involved.

Despite whatever efforts you plotted to keep her at arm's length, you now need her somewhat closer. Your good intentions and other cerebrations suddenly lie inoperative and obsolete. Their organ of origin, the brain, has given way to more insistent voices. You hear a chorus: Mexicans, your heart, your soul, your animal instincts all singing as one, "Live, live inside your body." And how can one resist a woman who, upon stepping into your room for the proffered siesta, kisses you and whispers in her absolutely best English, "Now we make pornográfico"?

Thus, with all the forces of nature and coincidence conspiring and compelling me, within a short span I had taken Adriana to comida and to supper, had on two occasions bought her beer at Mamma Mia's where we went to dance, and purchased for her a silk scarf she'd admired. Not great expenditures by gringo standards, but all beyond her means. While she accepted my invitations gracefully and without apology, I sensed she wished to reciprocate but, with a bare existence and a daughter to feed, could not do so easily. However, she soon devised a way.

One day I was sitting in the garden outside my room working on my tan and reading Remarque's *All Quiet on the Western Front*. Though his words described German soldiers who had survived the trenches, I felt them cut into me as if meant for my own American generation or, perhaps, any generation:

> Today we could pass through the scenes of our youth like travelers. We are burnt up by hard facts; like tradesmen we understand distinctions, and like butchers, necessities. We are no longer troubled—we are indifferent…We are forlorn like children, and experienced like old men, we are crude and sorrowful and superficial—I believe we are lost.

"¡Rico! ¡Rico!" I looked up. Lupe stood leaning on her cane at the steps beside the kitchen, in the passageway that funneled to the street. She lifted her chin and eyebrows and uttered in a dramatic stage whisper, "Hay una señorita a la puerta. Se llama Adriana."

"Gracias. I am coming."

I laid my book aside and grabbed my shirt. As I passed Lupe on my way to the door, she gave me an approving wink.

Net shopping-bag in hand, Adriana stood on the shaded banqueta in a sleeveless white blouse and her brown paisley skirt, one of two, seemingly, that she owned.

She elevated on her toes to kiss my cheek. "Can you come for supper?"

"Claro. ¿A qué hora?"

"A las siete."

"I'll bring some wine—red or white?"

She laid a hand on my forearm. "No, please. You have always invited me. Now I wish to invite you."

"Como tu quieras."

She smiled and moved off down the street toward the market. A charming invitation, but I wondered what dinner would be like. She didn't even have a stove.

*

The sun had just set as I moved down the dusky street where Adriana lived, following a garbage truck that ambled over the pocked roadway. With a wrench grasped in his left hand the driver clanged a steel plate hanging from his side-view mirror. At the sound, women came scurrying from behind stone walls carrying translucent pastel sacks. Through the thin plastic I could see coffee grounds, orange peels, and wadded paper. The women hefted the sacks onto the end of the slow-moving truck, where a pack of mongrels followed, sniffing and fighting over scraps that fell to earth.

I gazed to my left through open gates of the ramshackle homes on the north side of the street, dirt-floor shanties built of adobe and found objects. But even here, in the dusty yards where dogs, chickens, and children intermingled, I could see flowers growing from coffee tins and plastic buckets. Mature bougainvillea climbed through gerry-rigged electric wiring onto corrugated metal roofs, which told me these were not temporary dwellings, like refugee camps, where people awaited return home. This was it, this was home.

The women ferrying trash from these hovels to the creeping truck might have strutted from haciendas, for they all wore pressed cotton dresses, makeup, and jewelry, their hair coifed. All appeared well fed, healthy, and happy, calling to one another and laughing. I realized that despite their humble homes these were not the poor, not by Mexican standards. In Mexico the true poor were hungry and malnourished, like the campesinos who could not afford meat or eggs, or the elderly couple I'd seen rummaging for food in a dumpster at the market.

I rang the bell at the patio door. Soon I heard footsteps descending the metal stairs. Adriana's voice came muted through the door: "¿Quién?"

I whispered back: "A hungry and desperate man, capable of anything."

"Ah, perfecto." She opened the door and curtsied in a summery red dress. "Pásele, mi desperado."

In addition to the elegant dress, she wore a brass necklace circling her brown neck and long brass earrings dangling beneath the black hair that twined onto her shoulders. She offered me a braceleted hand to kiss. I bowed and did so.

As I stepped into her upstairs room I saw that she had fashioned a dining table from her workbench, over which she had draped a bright yellow cloth. In the center of it sat a lighted candle pressed into the neck of a Coca-Cola bottle. On either side of the candle lay two mismatched plates, knives and forks, a cup, and a glass. She offered me a tequila from a fresh half-liter of Oredáin. We drank our health, she from the cup, me from the glass.

Despite the ersatz table, chipped plates, and inelegant candle holder, despite the *patate de palma* that served as a bed, the bare walls, and the cardboard boxes on the floor, the room felt festive. But I realized that without Adriana and her red dress, without the fragrance of her perfume, without the brass necklace lying across her throat where I saw a faint throb with each beat of her heart, the room would not have seemed half so gay.

She invited me to sit across from her. For dinner she had prepared sautéed chicken on her cooking ring, which she served with a blanched broccoli salad and fresh *bolillos*, the hard dinner rolls local Mexicans favored. She had even bought a half-bottle of white wine. For desert she served fresh mango with cream and more tequila. Once again we toasted, touching cup to glass. After a silent minute she asked:

"¿Qué piensas?"

I looked up. "Sorry. I had gone away. Your home reminds me of my childhood and the rustic home we had on the lake. No telephone, no television. My father worked in town at the steel mill. We grew our own fruits and vegetables, trapped rabbits, fished and hunted. The best years."

"We need so little. Water, sun, some food, some love."

"That's why I keep returning to Mexico: It reminds me of my childhood; the people here remind me of my people. They work hard and never complain. They laugh and cry easily. They have a dignity and wariness I saw in my father."

At the word "padre," her features softened, her lips pressing together. She stared at the cup turning in her hand. After a moment she lifted her head.

"Mi padre…qué hombre. A soldier in the cavalry who had risen through the ranks to become an officer. What a handsome man in his uniform. No wonder my mother married him, even though she was a bourgeois and twenty years younger.

"He was nearly sixty when I was born but still taught me to ride, to shoot, to rope. He played records on an old phonograph and showed me the traditional dances. He strummed his guitar and sang songs from the revolution.

"He loved to drink with his friends, tell bawdy stories, and laugh. My mother would hide in shame. I remember, when we lived in Cuernavaca, my mother's bourgeois friends coming for a dinner party and my father greeting them at the door offering them his hand to kiss."

"He sounds like my father."

Her eyes glistened in the candlelight. She nodded. "I knew the first second I saw you. That's why I made sure we met. I looked at you and saw my father."

I poured us more tequila. She sipped, and her face hardened.

"He died when I was twelve. An hour after the funeral, my mother and aunt came into my room. Both were dressed in black with veils covering their eyes. 'Stop crying,' they ordered. There were to be no more such displays of emotion.

"They were like strangers. They frightened me. Their lips moved below the black veils as if suddenly they were blind. Things would be different now, my mother said. I didn't know what she meant. But I soon learned.

"There was to be no more music or dancing, no more horseback riding, no more laughter. The phonograph and records disappeared. She sold his guitar. For eight years she wore black. That was her revenge."

Adriana's eyes fixed on a dark corner of the room and

filled with tears. I reached across, took her hand, and pulled her to me. She rose, moved around the table, and slid onto my lap. I felt warm tears on my neck and her spare body trembling in my arms like a child's.

XV
Faith Healing

The Spanish-Moorish-Aztec architecture of San Miguel de Allende could grow oppressive. Stone and concrete walls everywhere: walled homes, walled gardens, abutting walls lining treeless streets. Broken bottles embedded in mortar atop walls exacerbated a sense of entrapment. You came to feel like a rat in a maze or an inmate in an asylum, thanks in part to a surfeit of crazy gringos, drug-addled, drunk, or just plain nutty.

To fight my feeling of imprisonment I'd take long walks in the surrounding countryside. But the arid, dusty terrain often brought little relief. You could feel just as trapped in a desert. However, at times these walks yielded surprising sights. Like the campesino I encountered on a trail astride his burro and wearing earphones, as if Mexico had skipped the machine age and gone straight from primitive agricultural into electronics.

Once, as I walked far outside town, I heard a tapping, like a woodpecker on a tin roof. I stopped and looked around but could not perceive its source. I continued on and heard more taps, two or three separate rhythms coming from beyond a ridge ahead of me. When I got to its top and gazed down the other side into a shallow valley I saw its source: A half-dozen brown men worked shirtless beneath the hot sun with hammers and chisels, rounding limestone piers into columns, smoothing slabs for steps or cornices, squaring paving stones. Under a thatched palapa, the only shade available in the quarry, stood a foreman studying blueprints. I thought of the pyramids at Teotihuacán and the quarrymen, their ancestors, who cut the stones.

Another time not far from town I moved through a parched field littered with bottles, cans, busted bricks, and paper diapers. Then I heard a flapping noise and turned to my right. On a rise lay a field of nopales, each spiny pad bearing the ubiquitous Mexican plastic sack handed out with every peso purchase, apparently wafted from the dump by westerly winds. They appeared to grow there, as if mad Mexican scientists had devised a succulent that bore such dubious fruit, and I imagined a line of bent campesinos moving through the field harvesting them.

One morning I woke feeling suffocated by the walls of San Miguel and the surrounding sand, longing for trees and the open road. My urge to break free if for only a day came upon me so strongly that I couldn't work, and after an hour gave it up. I grabbed my sweater and walked downhill to the jardín, crossing it toward the Salida de Dolores Hidalgo and Adriana's home. There the maid let me into the courtyard, where Angélica played with her doll and laundry dripped from stretched lines. I mounted the metal stairs and found Adriana at her workbench bent over a bracelet.

"I must get out of town before I go crazy," I told her. "Can you come with me to Guanajuato?"

She unplugged her soldering iron, stood, and spread her arms. "I am ready!"

And off we went.

It was at moments like this, and there were many, when despite her alluring femininity I saw the rugged influence of her father. Adriana was a soldier, always ready to de-camp and move out without fuss, to follow any order, to venture any campaign no matter how daunting. I saw him also in her iconoclastic humor: fanning herself immodestly with her skirt while strangers gawked at her brown legs, or climbing over the wrought-iron railing at an elegant side-walk café.

We carried Angélica to the *Jardín de Niños* then walked down the hill to the dusty plaza where buses stopped. With-in minutes we sat aboard a Flecha Amarilla bound for the state capital.

The bus headed off across a wide valley then up into wooded mountains. The narrow road climbed and twisted through pine forests and past scattered villages—usually no more than a few poor, flat-roofed dwellings and a confectionery. In the distance we could see an occasional home constructed on a mountaintop, including an incongruous Alpine chalet that looked more suited for the canton of Geneva than the state of Guanajuato. But mostly we gazed down into precipitous valleys, which the groaning bus hovered over as it careened onto the shoulder to avoid approaching vehicles materializing around blind turns.

At one point Adriana, who sat by the window, laid her hand on my mine and said, "Mira. There we are."

I lifted myself halfway out of my seat and followed her gaze down into a ravine where, two hundred feet below, lay a burned bus, the painted yellow arrow, the Flecha Amarilla, still visible on its flank. I felt my stomach rise and turned away.

Adriana smiled. "¿Tienes miedo?"

"Si. Heights scare me. It's genetic."

I told her the story of my father, from whom I inherited my acrophobia, and his one day of gainful employment during the Depression. His father, a steelworker with connections in the Polish community, arranged a job for him, a rare boon for a man barely twenty. He reported for duty and was hauled in a truck with other men to a North St. Louis munitions factory. There they were lifted on a rope-and-plank scaffold up the side of a hundred-foot-high chimney, which they were to clean with brushes, a government make-work project. As the others got busy, my father clung paralyzed to the smokestack. The foreman yelled from the ground: "Hey, you, get to work!" My father responded over his shoulder: "Fuck you!" They brought him down and gave him a day's pay, his only wages for the 1930's.

Within another hour the bus began winding down into a valley where lay Guanajuato, the most European of Mexican cities. Surrounding mines once supplied half the world's silver and funded the city's opulence. The Mecca of Mexican independence, Guanajuato was where Father Miguel Hidalgo led an army of campesinos armed with hoes, rakes, and homemade arms against Spaniards barricaded in the Alhóndiga de Granaditas, the public granary. The lad Pípila, now memorialized in a statue overlooking the city, tied a sandstone slab to his back to shield him from Spanish fire as he torched the wooden gate.

Most of the twisting streets, hemmed in by buildings running cheek-to-jowl on either side, lay too narrow for cars, so Guanajuato remained a largely pedestrian town. We meandered from the bus station past the Hidalgo Market and on to the small plaza at the Teatro Juárez. There we sat at a sidewalk café outside the Hotel San Francisco taking coffee and sweet rolls. From the open doors of the theater came the sound of a lone cello.

"This hotel"—I lifted my chin toward the building behind us—"is where a man I knew recently died."

Adriana sipped her café, her black-coffee eyes placid and content. There was much to be content about: the sun rising in a blue sky, leafy tamarind trees shading us, the earthy aroma of strong coffee, and the sweet taste of *pan dulce*; the twitterings of sparrows in the tamarinds, the pleasing façade of the theater, the soothing sound of the cello, and the leisure to sit at ease and drink it all in.

"¿De veras? ¿Cómo?"

"Tragically. He and his wife, two middle-age Americans living in San Miguel de Allende, came to Guanajuato for the weekend to see the mummies and Christ the King and visit the granary where Pípila burned the gates. They walked up and down the streets all day, had supper and wine at a restaurant, then returned to their room here at the Hotel San Francisco. Perhaps they made love. When she woke in the morning, her husband lay cold beside her. The doctor said he had had a heart attack.

"She knew no one here, had little money, and spoke little Spanish. The day before, she had seen the mummies and did not want him buried here to someday become a museum exhibit. So she had him cremated, and returned to San Miguel on the Sunday morning bus holding in her lap a cigar box with her husband's ashes."

Adriana took a bite of her sweet roll. "Death is everywhere."

"Claro," I agreed. But I didn't feel it. Adriana, sitting across from me with liquid eyes and moist, sugared lips, seemed the antithesis of death.

After breakfast we followed the sound of the cello inside

the theater, entering another age. Completed in 1903 and restored to its original splendor—an opulence that brought President Porfírio Díaz to its first performance—the compact Teatro Juarez outshone anything I had seen in Europe. Red velvet seats and curtains, crystal chandeliers, rococo gold leafing everywhere. On stage sat a lone cellist, the renown Mstislav Rostropovic, a handbill told us, who was to perform that evening. Dressed in a white shirt open at the neck and dark slacks, the balding musician bent over the instrument between his legs, moving his bow with an intense rhythm across its strings, rocking back and forth.

"Mira, Rick. He is making love to his cello."

"Sí. I thought the same."

His obvious rapture for his instrument and its powerful cry was so striking that I have carried that image of Rostropovic with me always, reminding me that to be an artist takes more than just technique—for a writer more than mere words and clever thoughts—but all one's ardor. Despite the required precision and devotion to the nuances of craft, there's nothing prissy or delicate about such work, which requires all heart and viscera. It is making love, making life.

Once again outside the theater, I asked Adriana, who had never before been to Guanajuato, what she wanted to see. "¿Las momias?"

The mummies of Guanajuato remain one of the most grotesque tourist attractions anywhere. While miners took great riches from the rocky soil surrounding Guanajuato, it was difficult to stick anything into it. So the dead were routinely assigned to crypts, rented for a period of years or eternity, depending on the means of the deceased's family. However, if and when the lease ran out, the tenant was turned out. But something about the climate of Guanajuato mummified the corpses. So families were then faced with the choice of coming up with more rent money or leaving the remains in the cemetery halls, where visitors paid a fee to view them.

"Have you seen them?" she asked.

I nodded.

"¿Qué pensaste?"

"Horrible."

"Pues, let's not. It is too beautiful a day to visit the dead."

"Then let's go to El Cubilete to see Christ the King."

She put her hand on my arm. "¿En serio?"

"Cómo no?"

"But how?"

"I will find a taxista who can give us a good fare. No problem."

"Entonces vámonos. I've always wanted to go, ever since my cousin was cured of cancer there."

I found a cabbie who was willing to negotiate, and together in the back seat Adriana and I soon headed off and up to El Cubilete and Christ the King.

The fifty-foot-high statue of *Cristo El Rey*, arms spread

in welcome and benediction, stood atop the mountain of El Cubilete overlooking Guanajuato, at a shrine where the infirm and crippled came for cures. Before the Spanish arrived, the site was held sacred by Chichimecs, who conducted human sacrifices there.

Our aged taxi tottered and banged over the rough, cobbled road that wound up the mountain, passing smoking school buses and pilgrims trekking the roadside. Near the top the road spiraled tight right, any deviation now checked by a stone wall, along which dilapidated buses waited for returning pilgrims. Our taxi parked beside the shrine.

As Adriana and I rose from the cab we noticed a young man with a useless, deformed foot swinging beneath him as he climbed back into a bus on crutches.

"No miracle for him," I said.

Adriana nodded. "Miracles must be rare to be miracles."

Though I had been to Guanajuato several times, I had never visited Cristo El Rey. Over the years I'd seen hundreds of shrines and churches in Mexico, France, Italy, Germany, and Spain. While I admired their beauty and solemnity, they all seemed much the same: The cathedral at Rheims reminded me of the one at Nuremberg; the one at Nuremberg reminded me of the Parroquia in San Miguel de Allende. But as we strode the last hundred yards to the zenith of El Cubilete, something singular swept over me.

At the low stone wall we stood gazing out over a vast valley, swirling wind buffeting us. Though the sun shone warm,

Adriana rubbed her bare arms. I felt it too. Maybe it was just the thinner air, for we had risen another thousand feet from Guanajuato, itself a mile high. Maybe that made me feel lightheaded and sense something chilling about the place. But here I am offering explanations I myself don't believe.

What I do believe is that the Chichimecs sacrificed humans there, that they cut out their hearts and ate them, like the Aztecs, or mutilated virgins and practiced blood orgies, and that somehow this history hangs in the air and is remembered in the black stone. When I subsequently returned to El Cubilete, the same eerie feeling again came to me.

The bending road emptied into a broad, stone plaza. There in the shadow of the looming figure of Christ, petitioners approached a shaded altar on their knees. One old Indian woman, black rebozo covering her head, rosary clutched in folded hands, moved inch by inch across the stones, tears coursing her crinkled brown cheeks. Following behind on his knees, gazing not at the altar but at Adriana, came her retarded, middle-aged son.

Others, unable to crawl in supplication, approached the shrine in wheelchairs, on crutches, or, like one pale woman, carried on a homemade stretcher. On the brick wall to the right of the altar hung casts, back braces, canes, and pink prostheses discarded, presumably, by those cured on the spot.

Adriana took my hand and led me inside, kneeling just to the left of the altar and a life-size Christ hanging crucified above it. I knelt beside her. She crossed herself, closed her eyes, and folded her hands, bringing them to her forehead. I looked from her to the wall adorned by the emblems of suffering to the suffering man above us. Though this was my first pilgrimage to Cristo El Rey, I had returned to Mexico time and again as if seeking a cure. Like those who believed in Christ the King, I sensed that this mystical land held healing powers for me. Yet how many actual cures were there? Thousands of petitioners came to the shrine every day, but only a score of prostheses hung on the wall. Perhaps that was my lot as well, symbolically to crawl across an endless plaza of hard stones praying for a miracle that might never come. Was that what faith was all about, not belief in a likely cure but simply the hope for one?

I looked from Christ back to Adriana, as still and beatific as a Madonna. Despite her travail and the hard life that likely lay ahead of her—far harder than I expected for myself—she remained full of hope, good cheer, and faith. Conversely, my faith in most everything had ceased, and I thus saw no use in wasting a futile prayer of petition on myself. Besides, I hadn't prayed to God since I was child and thought it a childish thing to do. Still, following Adriana's lead, I closed my eyes, folded my hands, and directed a prayer to Christ on her behalf, asking him to guide and protect both her and Angélica. As for me, I figured I could make it on my own.

XVI
An Emissary from God

In Mexico a strange reversal occurred within me over time. Previously, like most people, I had associated death with darkness and life with light. But now that had begun to invert.

This eclipse would seem unlikely given the sun-lit colors that marked the town: pastel yellow, green, and pink walls; purple jacarandas and magenta bougainvillea; blue skies, orange sunsets, tawny flesh. But death also seemed to reside in the light of day, in the arid sand and hard stones of the high desert, a sun-baked, desiccated earth that made me long for the lush, living hills of Missouri, for clear streams, tall trees, and cool rains. This, in comparison, seemed an inert land lying tombstoned with boulders, unquenched. Life, conversely, blossomed at night, like the moonflowers in Lupe's garden, where I heard things growing and moving in the dark. With the retreat of the killing sun the nocturnal air hung sweet, fertile, and vivifying. The darkness came alive, palpable, haunting and unsettling, like a bat.

Late one night as I walked past the park near the chorro, the spring where Indian women came to wash clothes, I heard chanting—a beseeching of dark gods, I surmised. But I could not be sure, for the words that wafted to me were neither Spanish nor English but seemingly indigenous Nahuatl: eerie, rhythmic, clear, and hypnotic, like the sound of a brook ambling over rocks. I sensed that this dark ritual, practiced under cover of night amid the thick trees that grew along the stream issuing from the spring, embodied a petition for life. I returned to my walled garden and slept reassured, as if in the arms of ancient gods. In those days the moon ruled me: I was drawn to it like a sun-beaten traveler seeking shade.

This embrace of darkness and the obscure, and wariness of light and the apparent, burgeoned on the hot day we retrieved Esperanza's body. As I now ponder it, I see how susceptible I was then, and to more than just ghosts and moonbeams.

I knew something was up the moment I stepped into Hal's apartment that morning. He opened the door wordlessly and motioned me inside with a nod. Hector stood leaning against the wall, Guillermo sat at the kitchen table, both silent. Before I could say a word or even shake hands, Hal came up behind me and spoke:

"Guillermo's wife died. Doctor Villareal killed her, but don't tell Guillermo that. If he knew, he'd slit the mother-

202 | RICK SKWIOT

fucker's throat…"

Guillermo might have overheard Hal, but neither he nor Hector spoke English. Both were taxi drivers who lived out in the countryside, sharing one taxi between them. I'd see Guillermo riding into town on his bicycle for his shift.

"…That's not all. The hospital won't give him her corpse till he pays the bill. A thousand bucks. He hardly makes that much in a year. Hector brought him here because he was talking crazy, talking about robbing a bank or kidnapping a gringo to get the cash."

I went over to Guillermo, took his hand, and gave him my condolences. He nodded and said, "It was God's will."

I sat across from him and turned to Hal. "What happened?"

Hal explained that Esperanza, three months pregnant with what would have been their fourth child, had a spontaneous abortion. When she wouldn't stop bleeding, Guillermo took her to Dr. Villareal. Villareal operated to stem the hemorrhaging but apparently didn't give her antibiotics. An infection set in that spread to her kidneys. After two days on a dialysis machine in the hospital at Celaya she died.

I shook my head. "When does he need the money?"

"Now. By law she has to buried within twenty-four hours. If he can't ransom her, they'll throw her in the fucking incinerator. He'd kill himself."

We sat silent. It was a lot of money for any of us. Despite being gringos, Hal and I were about as bad off financially as Mexican cabbies. I was living off the last of the money I'd earned freelancing in the States and would have to return north within weeks to get some more. Hal's royalties had dried up. He'd been reduced to writing implausible thrillers and Gothic romances under pseudonyms—Harriet Janeway was one—and living off a partial-disability check from the Army, since the Korean War had given him an ulcer. If anything, he was worse off than I was, borrowing money and selling off pieces of his next novel to any gullible gringo who happened into town. For a few hundred bucks he'd sign over ten or twenty percent of his "forthcoming" royalties, already mortgaging off perhaps six hundred percent of his next book.

Hal turned to me. "You got any money, man?"

Guillermo and Hector looked at me. Again I shook my head. "Lo siento. No tengo nada. Only enough to get home." They looked away.

Another silent minute passed. I studied Guillermo. He was even shorter than Hector and always wore cowboy boots and a high-crowned cowboy hat as if to hide it. But he appeared less Indian, more Spanish than Hector, with curling black hair and a prominent nose. We'd had a few beers together on occasion at Hal's. I rode with him in his taxi a couple times. A thoughtful, quiet, and self-conscious man. Once, I went with Hector to drop Guillermo at his home, moving through fields of asparagus, broccoli, sorghum, corn, and roses. He lived with his family in an adobe house in the campo, a home without running water or electricity that he himself had built. They grew a few vegetables and had a few goats. He rode his bicycle into town to drive a rented cab. A marginal existence at best. I could not imagine his life, its hardness and fragility. Now it seemed ready to break. If he could not bury his wife, he could never face his family, his friends, or himself.

"Tal vez…" I said, and stopped. Once again they looked at me. I spoke without thinking. "Tengo una tarjeta. Pero…" I turned to Hal and switched to English. "I have a credit card, but it's maxed out. Still, maybe the bank can't tell. Maybe we're far enough away."

It certainly seemed so to me. I felt far away from most everything.

*

Practically speaking, I was right. El Banco del Bajío was a long way from St. Louis and even further from being computerized. Luis, an assistant manager I sometimes drank with at La Cucaracha, didn't even bother to check the list to see if the card was stolen. He simply made out a credit-card slip by hand, had me sign it, and gave me the cash. It wasn't his problem, it was MasterCard's.

I came from the bank with the grand in my pocket. I could smell chorizo and cilantro frying under the portales across the jardín, where the Indian women cooked for travelers. The others sat waiting in the cab at the curb. I climbed into the back seat next to Guillermo and handed him the wad of cash. He nodded thanks and buttoned it into his shirt pocket.

We drove to a shop with a three-foot-long, child-size pine casket propping open the door, as if a macabre cognate to a barber pole. Through the door I could see two workers sawing and hammering. While Guillermo and Hector went inside, Hal and I waited in the taxi. He turned to me.

"Guillermo's my blood brother, and I got you into this. I'll pay you back soon as I get my advance."

I stared at a poster affixed to the wall of the carpenter's shop and festooned with clowns and tigers, announcing the arrival of the Circo Mágico in San Miguel de Allende. Hal probably meant it in a way. But it had been some time since his writing had earned him a dime, much less gotten him an advance. Also, he owed a lot of money around town to people he'd see every day, and I was soon leaving.

"I know," I said. But I had already written it off.

An old black station wagon reincarnated as a hearse, with black curtains on the side windows, pulled to the curb in front of us. The driver got out and went into the shop. Soon he and Hector came out carrying a wooden casket painted black, with rococo silver trim and tassels. They shoved it into the back of the hearse. Hector then slid behind the wheel of the cab. Guillermo again joined me in the back seat.

We followed the hearse to Celaya, the gaudy casket visible through its back window. I kept my eyes on the countryside, searching for something to comment upon to break the silence and cut the tension, or simply to divert Guillermo's gaze from the casket before us. Once, I spied a pair of horses about to mate. But then I caught myself and said nothing, reminded of Guillermo's loss.

The hospital was a new, one-story building near the town square. Inside, painters' scaffolds stood unmanned in the hallway. Sheets had been draped over doorways where doors had yet to be hung. In the lobby Guillermo embraced his mother, a small, sun-creased Indian woman with a black rebozo covering her head. He sat beside her on a wooden bench where, Hal said, she had spent the last two nights:

"She was afraid to leave. Afraid they'd think she was running out on the bill."

I leaned against the wall, smoking. A young woman in nurse's whites behind the front desk stared at me, gringos being less common in Celaya. When I stared back she looked away.

Guillermo moved to the desk and counted out the money. Then he motioned to me.

"Here, amigo. Count this for me. I'm too nervous."

I studied the bill but understood little about the charges. I checked the math, recounted the money, and handed it back to Guillermo. He passed it to the woman in white. She too counted it as Guillermo and I watched. Then, satisfied, she locked the cash in the desk drawer, lifted her chin, and said "Allí," indicating a glass door behind us.

We turned. Guillermo moved toward the door and stood silhouetted before it, feet spread, arms hanging loose. His mother came to his side. He reached for the handle. They entered the room holding hands and closed the door behind them. Through the glass I could hear their mumbled prayers. Hector, Hal, and I looked at one another and smoked in silence. Guillermo came out red-eyed, his arm around his mother. Hector motioned to me, and I followed him into the room.

Esperanza lay in a bloodstained, pastel-green dressing gown on a metal gurney: a young, round-faced woman looking very Indian and smelling of alcohol. With Hector at one end and me at the other we rolled the cart down a dark hallway and out the back door of the building, the others following.

We stepped into painful sunlight and a barren walled plaza of dusty earth. The hearse had been backed through metal gates that stood open. The incinerator sat to my left, next to oxygen bottles where the hearse driver stood blithely smoking a cigarette.

The ornate casket lay in the unbuffered sun on another gurney, next to which we wheeled Esperanza. Now, to lift the body into the casket. Hector held her shoulders. The hearse driver slid his arms under her back. I grabbed her ankles, lifeless and cold.

"Uno, dos, tres…"

We hefted her and lowered her into the black box. It

was then I noticed that on the inside of the lid in front of her face a mirror had been affixed, as if inviting her to stare into her own soul for eternity. I looked from the mirror to Esperanza and back again. A grackle snorted in a tree beyond the wall. I felt my stomach rise and turned away.

Guillermo moved to the casket. He gripped its edge, gazed down upon his wife, and threw back his head in a wild, wolf-like wail. It echoed off the hard earth and concrete walls, off the metal gurneys and the hearse, scraping down my spine and through my teeth. Then he collapsed across her body, enfolding her in his arms and whimpering like an animal caught in a trap. I stood by speechless and reached out to comfort Guillermo with a touch. But my Spanish was not good enough for this, or my English.

Hector went to him and pulled him away. "Ven, amigo. You can see her later."

Guillermo's mother left in the hearse with Esperanza and the driver. Hal, the two cabbies, and I walked back through the hospital and out onto the street. Across the cobblestones in the shade of a facing building stood an old man selling cubed watermelon in plastic cups.

"¿Sandía?" Hal asked, and we crossed the street.

We leaned against the cool, shaded wall, eating the red flesh with toothpicks. After a minute, along the sidewalk before us glided a man, half a man, who had been shorn below the waist. Pushing gloved fists against the sidewalk he propelled himself on the base of a shopping cart, the cart, too, having been sawn in half.

Guillermo smiled and greeted the man as he passed then eyed his progress down the block. "¡Qué hombre!" Guillermo said, shaking his head in admiration. "There's not even a supermarket within a hundred miles."

*

The next morning was like the last and the one before it: an unfettered sun burning through thin mountain air and parching the earth. The Parroquia was packed with mourners. In the back women wept openly as at the altar Guillermo and Esperanza had returned to the spot where they were wed. I stood against the back wall near two infants crawling on the floor. The little girl reached out her hand. Cautiously the little boy took it. I slipped out the door fearing I, too, might weep.

I found Hal and Hector in the jardín. As the cortege came from the church and moved solemnly on foot toward the Panteón, we slid into Hector's taxi and moved off.

Not the time of day or type of day to be drinking tequila, I thought. Nonetheless, when Hal passed me the plastic bottle of cheap liquor over the front seat of the cab, I took a swig. Hector pushed a tape in, and the lilting accordion of ranchera music seeped from the speaker, a song that spoke of lost love, despair, and true lovers meeting in heaven.

We circumnavigated the cortege, rode down the Ancha de San Antonio, and stopped alongside three other green-and-white taxis outside the walls of the Panteón. Through the opened gates I could see low marble crypts resting in the shade of tall pines and, further down the hill, concrete crypts built four-high in a treeless, dusty field. Beside one such shadeless crypt a lone sexton waited.

We stepped from the cab and looked back up the road. The cortege snaked down the hill from the *centro*, a ten-wide phalanx of campesinos and mestizos marching in a cloud of dust behind the black hearse.

I shook hands with Julio, a young dentist who rode about town on his son's undersized bicycle making deliveries, clear plastic baggies of repaired dentures in his grasp. I'd been to his house once for comida and was served roast goat in a parlor that doubled as dining room and dentist's surgery. Afterward I had enjoyed a tequila reclining in the dental chair where Julio drilled on his patients.

As the cortege crept near, the incongruous sound of a march, sprightly and tinny, abruptly blared over the hill behind us. We turned. Skipping into town from the other direction came clowns, acrobats, and jugglers leading a flatbed truck on which an elephant and camel had been tethered and where a caged tiger paced. The music screeched from a loudspeaker on the truck's roof. A sign on its door announced the arrival of the Circo Mágico. Then, as the truck driver noticed the cortege approaching from the opposite direction, he killed the music. The two processions passed shoulder-to-shoulder. The clowns hung their heads and assumed a solemn pace. The black-clad mourners, tears momentarily abating, gazed with curiosity at the colorful characters and exotic animals. Then, when they parted, the music again began to play, the clowns to skip, the mourners to weep.

The hearse reached the cemetery gates. A sudden blast from the horns of the taxis behind me made me start. The tribute persisted, sounding like a moan from the grave, as the black station wagon ground past us through the dust. Guillermo, dressed in black jeans and black cowboy shirt, stumbled blindly behind, sobbing, face buried in the crook of his left arm, his right hand reaching out as if to grasp the hearse, to yank the casket from it and bar his wife from entering the city of the dead. His mother followed two paces back in the same posture with arm outstretched, black shawl covering her head, appearing like a shadow of death pointing the way. The horns blared on, and Julio, who stood beside me, held himself and shivered.

We fell in at the end of the cortege and marched down the hill, where the crypt stood like a black mouth waiting to consume Esperanza. When the mourners had gathered round it, the fair-skinned priest from the Parroquia stood before them mouthing words that a breeze carried aloft before reaching me.

Julio saw me studying a mound of broken, decaying coffins stacked against the cemetery's back wall. He leaned over and whispered, "No pagaron la renta," then made a digging gesture to suggest disinterment for not making payments.

When the priest finished, the pallbearers lifted the ornate black casket and slid it into the crypt. The waiting sexton, a grizzled old man with rope belt, stepped onto a low stool and began closing the crypt with bricks and mortar. The mourners gazed in silence, the only sounds the plopping of wet concrete and the scraping of his trowel. When the bricks were in place, the old man smoothed mortar over them. Guillermo stepped forward and handed him a piece of paper.

From it the gravedigger copied the name and dates of Esperanza Morales Campos into the wet concrete with his index finger, though impressing the esses backward. When he finished, Guillermo again approached the crypt, placing a single rose on the ledge below her name. The mourners turned away.

I moved off alone to a square of green earth I had spied in the center of the arid cemetery, marked by a wrought-iron fence. The Episcopalian plot, a sign there noted. A cemetery within a cemetery, where expatriate Brits, Canadians, and Americans were buried. One stone indicated a man roughly my father's age, and I thought of his grassy grave in moist Missouri soil. A black cloud of longing and loss passed over me, not only for him but for my home and for myself. I had cut myself off and knew not my purpose or where I belonged—but I knew not here, not for eternity. The thought of being buried in the hard earth of this strange land, perhaps one day to be dug up and thrown out with the banana peels and broken Coke bottles, chilled me.

"Señor…Señor…"

I turned.

Guillermo's mother stood five paces away clutching a rosary, her black rebozo still covering her head. Guillermo hovered behind her. She stepped toward me, trembling hands folded as if in prayer.

"Gracias. Muchas gracias, señor."

"De nada, señora. For nothing."

"Estabas…estabas enviado por Dios."

I took her rough hand in mine and shook my head. "No, I do not believe so."

"No, it is the truth. You were sent by God."

XVII
The Death of Rico Verdoso

Sitting in the sling chair among the plants outside my door, I read through a scene I had written upon rising and laid it aside. Though not yet noon, it was a good day's work. So I decided to abandon my novel for now and focus on other than cerebral pursuits, to live inside my body.

Earlier Hal had predicted that as I developed as a writer, the real world would no longer hold for me the enchantment of my created fictional worlds. That had yet come to pass though it would later, at least in spurts, when my real world lay gray and monotone. But here, with its vibrant colors, piquant aromas, chiming church bells, and warm sun, Mexico kept urging me to seek my salvation through the senses, and I obeyed.

First though I wanted to send a note home to Romana, who was often in my thoughts. I pulled from my journal a picture postcard I had bought the previous day at the jardín, haunted by its scene: Puffy white clouds sat in blue sky above the dark mountains of Guanajuato; in the foreground lay a green valley and an aquamarine lake; the arching branch of a purple-flowering jacaranda tree, presumably held in front of the camera by a creative photographer, helped frame the picture. It was a scene of great beauty but with a sense of mystery I could not explain.

On the verso I wrote a brief note telling how clear the air hung on this bright morning, as clear as that in the photo, and how I missed the green hills and home. I signed it and turned it over to study the scene once more, and suddenly realized what made the picture so eerie: The clouds were upside down. Flat and grayish on top, puffy and white on the bottom. Only in surreal Mexico. Our creative photographer, trying to add some interest to a naked blue sky, stripped in clouds from another shot. But in a slapdash Mexican way, he did it all *chingado*.

I flipped the card over and added a P.S.: "Look above the mountains: nubes invertidas, emblematic of my strange life here."

After lunch I slipped my feet into my sandals, grabbed the postcard, and strode across the garden toward the street. With few exceptions, I still ate my meals at Anglo-Saxon, not Hispanic, hours. But then I rose at an Anglo-Saxon time when most Mexicans still had hours of sleep in them. Once, when staying at the Posada Carmina upon first returning to town, I told the morning waiter that I'd like coffee brought to my room at seven a.m. the next day. He frowned uncomprehendingly and asked, "What for?"

As a result of my gringo schedule I still had an hour in which to run errands before everything closed down for three hours to accommodate comida and siesta. I moved down the Calle de Correo, the Street of the Post Office, on which I lived. Like virtually every street in the centro it ran downhill and resembled a great stone trough. The walls of the houses abutted one another and pressed to the stone sidewalk on either side of the flagstone street. No alleys or trees, no front lawns or porches. Wrought-iron bars covered what few, shuttered windows faced the street.

Down the block, just this side of the post office, a tall wooden ladder leaned against a home. Atop it a lean, young, bareheaded mestizo applied peach-colored paint to the stucco wall with a wide brush. The walls of San Miguel de Allende came mostly in pastels: peach, apricot, lemon, and lime; sand, sky blue, ochre, and rust, often trimmed in a darker, complementary hue. With bright mountain sun every day, the effect was cheery and pleasing. But as I approached the painter I noticed that a well-dressed middle-age Mexican couple stood in the street scolding him, judging by their gestures. When I got within earshot I heard the woman say:

"Mira, joven. Don't you see what you are doing? Your paint is flying all over our blue wall. We had it painted just last year. You must clean it up now."

The dark young man on the ladder turned, brush in hand. "Claro, señora. When I finish here I will move my ladder and erase all the splatters with turpentine. Your wall will not be harmed."

He started to turn back to his work, but the woman went on: "By then the paint will be dry. You will ruin our wall. You must remove it now while it is still wet."

"It will be fine, I promise. I have painted a hundred walls."

Those words prompted the portly husband to lurch forward and shake the ladder, causing the painter to grab onto the top of the wall.

"Don't argue with the lady. Come down now and do as she says."

The painter glared down at the man. He replaced his brush in the paint can hanging from the ladder and backed down the rungs. When he reached the street the couple started gesturing at the wall again.

"Look at this. I demand that you clean it up now," bellowed the husband.

When I saw the way the painter looked at the man, chin lowered, with a steady black gaze, I stopped. He wiped his hands on a paint-smeared bandana that he took from his back pocket.

"Permit me to explain. If I clean it up now, I will only have to clean it again when…"

"Don't give me your excuses, peasant. Clean it now or

I'll see you'll never paint another wall in San Miguel."

With that the painter turned away, muttering. The older man threw a fist and caught him just behind the ear. The painter whirled and backed away, arms loose at his sides. The other advanced swinging wildly, punches that the painter easily slipped retreating and turning his shoulders left or right. They danced across the street and back again, the painter waltzing smoothly, the fat man stiff-legged, turning red and cursing, his wife wringing her hands.

Then as if on cue two *policías* came sauntering around the corner of the post office. When they saw the men the cops halted but an instant, as if doing a synchronized dance of their own, then continued forward at the same leisurely pace but now tapping their nightsticks in the palms of their hands, a steady plap, plap, plap echoing their footsteps on the street.

The older officer called out in a singsong voice, "Jóvenes, jóvenes. ¿Qué pasa, youngsters?" At his words the two men froze.

Moments like this, I would think, made life as a San Miguel policeman bearable. New hires were given a nightstick, a badge, and a blue cap, and made to walk the hilly, cobbled streets in twelve-hour shifts, six a week, for thirty-five dollars American. But the prestige and power on occasions such as this must have been priceless for someone near the bottom of the social totem-pole. For awhile you got to sit on someone else's head.

The younger cop, a slow-eyed Mayan-looking fellow with a bad haircut, moved between the two contestants, facing the painter, nightstick grasped at either end in crowd-control posture. His partner took the boxer aside and listened intently to his tale, and to the importuning of his wife, stroking his chin, pursing his lips, and nodding. After perhaps a minute he turned to the young cop and called:

"Pedrito: Traígale."

With that, Pedrito turned the painter around and secured his wrists in gleaming handcuffs, *esposas*, the Mexicans called them: wives. With a cop on either side, the painter was marched off toward the Presidencia.

As they passed I said, "Oye, señores…," to begin to explain what really had happened. But the older cop just flicked his eyes at me with a hard gaze that silenced me, and they kept on walking. The couple retreated into their home. I was left standing in the street, along with the ladder.

After I mailed my postcard I walked down the Salida de Dolores Hidalgo and turned right on the street where Adriana lived. As I did I saw her coming out of her door with Angélica's hand in hers and a package under her arm.

We touched cheeks as we met. Angélica looked up and stretched out her arms toward me. "Señor Rico, llévame por favor."

I lifted her in my arms and fell in step beside Adriana.

"¿A dónde vas?" I asked.

"Al correo. I need to mail these bracelets to a shop in De

Efe. Then to the market to buy Angélica a bird."

She showed me the box of bracelets, handsome creations of twisted copper fettuccine, which I complimented. But as we walked on I fell silent.

"¿Qué piensas?" she asked. "Something's on your mind."

I told her about the incident I had just witnessed in the street and asked: "Please go with me to the Presidencia to help explain. The police don't listen to gringos."

"To explain what?"

"That they have arrested the wrong man."

Adriana lay her hand on my forearm as we strolled up the hill toward the jardín. "No, no, mi Rambo. They have arrested the correct man: the worker, the Indian, and not the burgués."

"But he did nothing illegal. It's the other cabrón who should be in jail for assault."

"Perhaps. But here the rich man can buy his way out of jail no matter whom he has killed while the poor man sits in the bote for nothing and rots. In this case, however, little damage is done. The painter will spend a night sleeping on the floor of the jail, and the rich neighbor will save face. Tomorrow the young man will be back at his job and left to perform it as he sees fit. Watch and see."

I shook my head. "It seems so feudal. There is no justice."

We moved under the trees of the jardín, crossing to the Calle de Correo. But halfway across the square I stopped and grabbed her hand.

"Come. I want to show you something."

The three of us circled back around the jardín and halted under an elm with white-painted trunk. I lifted my chin toward a metal bench in the shade. "Mira. There they are."

The couple with the paint-splattered house sat with sour expressions at either end of the bench, staring off in opposite directions, looking like a pair of disgruntled Buddhas.

Adriana smiled. "There is your justice."

While she went to mail her package I bought Angélica a *paleta*, a Mexican popsicle, under the portales and listened to her tell of the little bird she wanted for her pet. I was easily charmed by other people's children, for whom I could buy treats and play the beneficent uncle without having to house, feed, or discipline them. But a four-year-old girl sporting her mother's dark eyes, wearing a bright cotton dress, and speaking in a musical little voice of her "paraquito verde" that she would love "con todo de mi corazón" was a charmer few could resist.

Soon Adriana found us, and we marched off together toward the mercado. There, in a square just outside the market, bordered on one side by yet another of San Miguel's myriad churches, we moved under colorful cloths Indian women had strung against the penetrating mountain sun. We wended among makeshift stalls of cooking utensils, used American clothing, fruits, and vegetables. Dressed chickens hung from lines and live ones, along with black ducks, sat waiting in wooden cells. Soon we came to the exotic birds that jungle Indians netted and housed in bamboo cages: warblers, cockatoos, toucans, and macaws, blue, red, and yellow. But Angélica moved directly to a cage containing a little green parakeet.

"Here he is: Rico Verdoso."

I felt Adriana's eyes on me. Greenish Rick: The kid had named her bird after me, the pet she had promised to love with all her heart. These damn Mexicans were insidious, like a virus. They kept getting under your skin, infecting you, even when you were doing your best to remain detached.

Outside the market I took Adriana's hand. "I think there's salsa tonight at Mamma Mia's. Do you want to dance?"

"Of course."

"Come to my place first." I looked to Angélica cradling the bamboo birdcage in her arms, then back to her mother. "For a drink."

Adriana nodded and smiled shyly. "With much pleasure."

"Como siempre."

After we parted I retreated to the jardín to buy some watermelon before my siesta. There the old woman handed me a plastic cup of red fruit from her cart near the Parroquia. I sauntered toward a bench under the elms of the jardín, spearing a cube with a toothpick.

"Hey, Rick! Ven acá."

I looked up to see Arturo, the artist, sitting on a bench and waving me over with a magazine. We shook hands, and I lowered myself beside him. He lifted the magazine and chortled.

"Some gringo left this at the coffee shop. Listen: 'Can Terrorism Ruin Your Vacation?' Ha ha. 'A Silent Killer May Lurk in Your Home: Radon.' Too funny." He turned another page and read: "'Designer Diseases: The New Japanese Import.' This is killing me." He wiped tears of mirth from his eyes. "Do gringos really worry about all this mierda?"

"Fear sells."

"I am sorry, amigo. I know Mexico is bien chingado, but your land is really fucked up, though amusing. Let fear guide you and you become zombies, the living dead."

Chewing on a piece of melon, I lifted my chin toward his magazine. "You don't know the half of it…" I went on to tell him of paper sashes on toilet seats, government health-warnings on beer bottles and cigarettes, and non-smoking sections in restaurants. Of auto-emissions inspections, seat-belt laws and mandated smoke-detectors.

Holding his sides and turning red with glee, Arturo rose from the bench. "Stop, Rick. I can't take any more. I must go paint it."

*

I slept for an hour then went to the patio with my journal and a copy of *Leaves of Grass* under my arm. I took a limón from a branch, squeezed it into a cup of tea, and settled back in the sling chair under a papaya tree.

From my journal I took the sheets of typescript I had written that morning. Pencil in hand I read through them again, paring language, adding sensory details, choosing a better word. At the time I thought I was doing great work. As it turned out, the pages were part of a training novel that readers would never see. Still, it was a labor of love that paid benefits: telling me how to approach my work, teaching me daily discipline, showing me I could do it.

Next I wrote in my journal about the house-painting incident and finding the bored bourgeois couple in the jardín. Then I turned to Walt Whitman.

I remember this time of my life fondly in numerous contexts, but one great pleasure that still reverberates was my reading. Thanks to the bilingual library of San Miguel, stocked in large part from the estates of departed Anglophone residents, I became better acquainted with writers who have remained mentors and companions. Part of the library's richness came from its plethora of classics. It also contained books by contemporary writers, donated by people who perhaps belonged to book clubs, but these I avoided, sticking with Fitzgerald, Chekhov, Cather, Homer, Whitman, and their ilk.

For some reason I had previously avoided Whitman. My father kept a copy of *Leaves of Grass* on his bookshelf, the only poetry there other than Baudelaire's *The Flowers of Evil* and Shakespeare's. Odd choices, perhaps, for a steelworker, but he had spent some ten unemployed Depression years at the Central Library in St. Louis, where librarians guided his reading. I had likely peered into his Whitman as a child, found it incomprehensible, and never went back. I had had no idea that he belonged to the same club as Emerson, Thoreau, Henry Miller, and D.H. Lawrence, the Transcendentalists Club, which, encouraged by the deeply intuitive Mexicans I'd encountered, I now wished to join. As the sun fell behind the wall, I copied into my journal Whitman's line: "Ever the bandage under the chin, ever the trestles of death." It was then that I heard a voice:

"Rico…Tsst…Rico."

I looked up. Lupe was at her kitchen window, alight now as dusk approached. She made a beckoning gesture. "Ven."

I laid my journal aside, crossed the garden, and moved down the three steps to her kitchen. At the table sat her son Alfredo, the doctor, whom I had met but once in passing when he visited from nearby Irapuato with his wife and children. We shook hands. Lupe ordered me to sit and poured me a tall shot glass of tequila. Alfredo already had one in front of him.

"Alfredo's come like St. Christopher to carry Christ," she explained.

"Ah, sí. Para Semana Santa."

I would see this San Miguel de Allende Holy Week ritual the following day. On Good Friday six men carried a life-size and lifelike bleeding replica of Jesus enclosed in a glass casket through the streets of the hilly pueblo. Pacing with solemn faces in the hot sun, they moved from a church on the lower side of town up the hill and past the market, circling through throngs pressing to see the martyr and arriving finally at La Parroquia on the jardín. The procession, accompanied by the doleful music of a brass band, took hours.

Lupe sat between us. "When Alfredo passes I smile and wave from the crowd to see if I can break his mask." Lupe mimicked Alfredo's dour official expression and then acted out her role.

Alfredo turned to me. "Mi madre es una pagana. Well, so am I. All Mexicans are pagans at heart. Here. More tequila."

Alfredo poured us both another shot and tried to fill his mother's glass as well, but she waved him away. He insisted: "It's me, not you, that has to march with the Christians in the sun tomorrow. For the love of Jesus have another."

"How can I drink without music? Go get your guitar, hijo."

Alfredo, dark-bearded and thick, pushed up from the table and moved into the adjoining *sala*. I heard his footsteps on the stone stairs that led up to the bedrooms. Soon he returned with a polished, ochre instrument. Once again he sat across the table from me, tuning it.

"Alfredo is good with catgut," Lupe said, "from sewing

up his patients."

"My mother is making jokes." He switched momentarily to English: "I'm an internist, not a surgeon. Like a witch doctor. We don't have all the sophisticated equipment, the MRIs, the CAT scans, and the rest. So you ask and you listen. You touch and you divine. It is more art than science."

He strummed a chord and fell silent. Then with another stroke he began to sing in a full, penetrating voice that echoed off the stucco walls. He sang a plaintive ballad I did not know, a song, like many Mexican songs, of lost love and great longing.

When he finished, Lupe and I applauded. Alfredo took the instrument by the neck and handed it across the table. "Okay, your turn."

I protested: "I haven't played in years…I can't remember any songs…My voice is terrible…" All pretty much true. But this was a Mexican party, at which everyone sings, everyone dances, everyone drinks and enjoys himself—no excuses!

Alfredo still held the guitar out. "Take it."

"¡Cante, Rico!" Lupe added in her authoritative, school-teacher voice.

I took the guitar, held it on my lap, and bit my lip. I stroked it quietly. "Let me think. Maybe I can remember one…"

I played a few opening chords, B-flat, D, A, F, and it came back to me. I sang:

> They say everything can be replaced,
>
> They say every distance is not near,
>
> So I remember every face
>
> Of every man who put me here.

Alfredo translated on the fly, whispering Bob Dylan's words in Spanish to his mother after each phrase.

I managed to get through the three verses with hardly a hitch. The chorus came automatically:

> I see my light come shining
>
> From the west down to the east.
>
> Any day now, any day now,
>
> I shall be released.

Alfredo went on to a cantina to meet with old friends and fellow pallbearers. I went back to my room. Soon I heard the electric bell at the door to the street. There I found Adriana in turquoise blouse and tight blue jeans. A silver necklace shone against her bronze throat.

Lupe's kitchen lay dark as we passed. The garden was lit by the electric bulb outside my door, above which magenta bougainvillea clung to the white wall, where a brown scorpion crawled up from the stack of firewood.

Once inside I drew the curtain across the doorway and lit a candle on the mantel. I took the bottle of Oredáin and poured two fingers worth into two glasses. Standing before the mantel we knocked the drinks together, drank, and kissed, Adriana tasting of lipstick and tequila. A breeze ruffled the curtain over the doorway and rippled the flame of the candle.

*

Adriana and I were sitting side-by-side on my bed, leaning against the stucco wall as I read from my typescript in light falling from the bedside lamp. I was reading the English words in my head but speaking them aloud in Spanish as best I could. Adriana's cheek pressed against my shoulder as I described the subway in Mexico City snaking past the remains of buried temples and pyramids while, on the streets above, millions of *la raza*, the new, postcolonial race neither wholly Indian nor Spanish, moved about over the bones of their ancestors.

Soon we dressed and moved arm-in-arm across the patio, down the three steps, and into the street, which lay dark beneath a new moon. Just before reaching the jardín I heard drifting down from a rooftop bar the sound of trumpets and men singing. Atop the two-story building we saw the wide sombreros of a mariachi band. I thought of Alfredo and wondered if he was among the revelers.

In candlelit Mamma Mia's the band had just taken the small stage. Adriana and I leaned against the bar drinking beer. Amid a crowd of perhaps thirty customers I spied Arturo sitting alone on the far side of the room, holding a beer bottle and staring at the floor. I waved but he did not see me. Perhaps he was thinking of his canvas on American fear.

Soon a lanky flautist stepped to the microphone to blow a few notes, and the band came to life behind him. The short, Peruvian-looking percussionist beat his palms on deep drums; the acoustic-guitarist strummed piercing chords; a thickset young man thumped an old double bass. The song seemed more samba than salsa, smooth and lilting. Yet none of the couples moved to the small dance floor in front of the band.

But soon I saw Arturo rise and step to the empty floor. He clutched his beer bottle to his chest as if his beloved and danced toward us, eyes closed. At the edge of the dance floor he whirled, shook his shoulders, and sidled back. There he paused dramatically, did a one-eighty, and sambaed our way again.

Someone just coming into town from, say, New York might have thought him part of the floorshow. But no one in the band or the audience except me seemed to pay him any mind. Despite its Spanish courtesies and formal traditions, and despite being a police state, Mexico was free in ways other lands were not. Behavior that might raise eyebrows or bring derision in Houston, London, or Lyon passed here without comment. Arturo clearly did not care that others might think him vain, exhibitionistic, drunk, or crazy for dancing alone in such a histrionic way. Likewise, other patrons and the management were indifferent to his performance. In Mexico the guiding principle for much behavior seemed to be not propriety or precedent but individual need, good form less important than fulfilling one's wants and getting the job done. Thus, bizarre individual variations were accepted in most everything: architecture, dress, lovemaking, dancing.

Further, Arturo's impatience, his refusal to wait for an unattached woman to accompany him to the dance floor or for other dancers to shield him from view, was also typically Mexican. Why wait? He wanted to dance now. Life is short, death eternal.

So what was I waiting for? I took Adriana by the hand and headed to the dance floor.

*

After midnight we strolled down the middle of the quiet Salida de Dolores Hidalgo. Outside The Ring, a disco that stayed open till five, we bid, "Buenas noches," to the bouncer as we passed. Just steps beyond, from a young man with a propane grill mounted on a bicycle-wheeled cart, we bought two *hamburguesas* on *pan Bimbo* and ate as we walked.

The town lay silent and dark. Beyond the occasional streetlight the night sky hung starry and black. We were nowhere: out in the hinterlands of a Third World country, far from the din, hurry, and angst of the life I had long known. Yet I felt so much at home.

Adriana walked beside me, gazing up at the stars. "Qué noche," she said. "Qué bella."

I nodded agreement but thought, "Qué dia," and how beautiful *it* had been—how rich, fortifying and full of life.

We turned onto the Calzada de La Luz. At her home I waited outside Claudia's door as Adriana went in. I heard them speaking, and soon Adriana emerged with Angélica in her arms, fast asleep. I took her from her mother, her soft little body warm against me, and followed Adriana through the patio door and up the stairs.

Adriana unlocked her door. Inside the dim room I placed Angélica on the palm mat where she slept beside her mother and pulled a blanket over her. When I turned, Adriana stood frozen in front of the bamboo birdcage resting on her workbench. I moved beside her and gazed down. There, on the floor of the cage, lay Rico Verdoso.

"¿Está muerto?" I asked.

"Suficiente," she replied.

I shook my head. "Poor Angélica."

Adriana lifted her chin toward the cage. "Pobre Rico Verdoso."

I moved back up the Salida de Dolores Hidalgo thinking again about death, however, not as a dreaded evil as I once had but as a necessary frame for life and a call to action. Sooner or later it would have its day. Meanwhile I needed to make the most of what was given, to live large or die trying.

I knew I would have to head north shortly, for I was again living off borrowed money to prolong my stay. I prayed that I would be able to return soon. Thanks to Mexico I had begun again to live inside my body, to live with my heart and my senses and less so merely inside my mind. But with Mexicans, you can't do otherwise. They simply won't allow it.

Perhaps, as Licha said, to be a true Mexican, or truly human, one must be able to make love with people watching, figuratively speaking. That is, to abandon yourself to your desires wholeheartedly no matter what others may think. Like Arturo, you have to dance with yourself and, like Adriana, to be ready at all times. From them and all the others, Ernesto, Daniel, Ilena, and more, I was taught to obey my gods and my heart and hope for the best. To be grateful for small blessings and accepting of hard lessons. To realize that when things, inevitably, don't turn out as planned, to shrug and say, "Ni modo."

EPILOGUE

Twenty Years After

At La Cucaracha cantina I order a tequila straight up, served in a small tumbler filled to the brim. At the far end of the bar a familiar face. A name comes floating back from deep memory: Chucho. He spies me and nods. Some twenty years have passed since we were teammates playing on the concrete basketball court at Parque Juárez, but we recognize each other. I feel as if I have never left.

From Chucho and the young bartender, Hernán, I learn of Ernesto's passing two years earlier from cancer. But he was still the same until the end, Chucho says, full of life and high spirits, of goodwill and laughter. ¡Qué hombre!

We start buying rounds. After a couple more tumblers of Hornitos, and after Chucho is fetched home by his teenage daughter, I retreat into my own swirling thoughts. I sit wondering at the fragility of life and of memory. Earlier that day I had encountered Lupe, my dueña for many years, on her doorstep. She looked much the same but clearly was not. She had no recollection of me, or of the American woman who died in the apartment upstairs or of others who had lived there. "My memory is not good these days," she admitted.

But my memory this night is perhaps too good. I remember Ernesto and his kindnesses: the times he took me out on the town, the cane he brought me as a gift when I broke my ankle, his generosity of spirit. I see him standing beside me at the bar there, entreating me, as he would, to write his life's story, and feel his ample humanity and its absence. I should have been here, I tell myself. Missed him by just two years. I should have been here.

Once, I felt I belonged. But I abandoned it all, chasing whatever I was chasing, and am still chasing. A deep longing for the life I left unlived in San Miguel washes over me. *La vida pasando.* Life goes on. And as each instant passes, "now" is lost forever. People die and with them all sensation and recollection vanish, life deeply felt, acknowledged and cherished. Or memory fails. Then after we're gone what remains but a few photographs where, after a brief time, no one will be able to identify us? And thus all the affecting and resonant moments of life, the tumult of feeling, dies with us. Which is why one writes a memoir, I see through my tequila haze. To be a historian of the unhistoried, to borrow Proust's phrase. To put celebrity and its corrupting influence in their proper place, recording and preserving struggles, dilemmas, and courage just as great as that of "great" people.

*

I had ended up back in San Miguel de Allende on a rational journey. I thought that to bring closure to this memoir and give it some contemporary context I should make a return visit to the scene of my experiences exactly twenty-five years after my first sojourn there. But my trip did nothing to bring closure. Instead, as with all my previous trips to Mexico, I came away with strange doors opening, with a sense of being infected by the haunting spirit of the land and the staunch humanity of its people. I felt myself being seduced by Mexico and Mexicans all over again.

It began even before I left. I called to make arrangements for an apartment, trotting out my rusty Spanish to chat long distance with my future landlord, Miguel Olvera García. Speaking with him—polite, soft-spoken, dignified—I was reminded how welcoming and solid the people were, making each visit feel like a homecoming. In Mexico, Old World charm and propriety still exist—a precise formality, substantial and light at the same time; life with the out-of-bounds clearly marked—recalling to me my childhood under the watchful eyes of my first- and second-generation American parents, people steeped in European folkways. Miguel also reminded me of Lupe, the Lupe of old, with her intellectual playfulness and moral certainty. Though not a censorious, prudish morality but one based on civility and community. When I suggested sending a deposit, Miguel declined, saying it wasn't necessary, trusting me as Lupe had twenty-five years earlier.

Upon arriving I find that the country remains much the same as always, the typical Mexican mix of surface chaos and fundamental order. At the airport in De Efe it takes me an hour to get through customs, though others on my flight are whisked through in minutes thanks to the whimsy of officials directing human traffic there. Outside the airport I spy large, colorful tapestries and futuristic advertisements erected to hide the makeshift homes, disorder and gritty Third World reality just yards away. I grab a cab to take me to the north bus station, as I had on my first trip to San Miguel.

The capital seems as exotic and anarchic as ever: dirty, smoggy, smelly, vibrant, intoxicating. Sensory and psychic overload: Men overhauling auto engines in the street. A billboard with a photo of a newborn, announcing Caesarean sections for 7,500 pesos. A local bus with only women passengers and a sign reading, "*Solo damas.*" On the outskirts, jerry-rigged hovels housing families far removed from the luxury of Polanco, just minutes away.

A five-hour bus ride, much of it through torrential rains. An unkempt country: trash, derelict vehicles and half-finished homes everywhere, signaling, perhaps, reality outracing hope (or a counterproductive property-tax that climbs precipitously when structures are completed). Buses ubiquitous: Despite its bountiful natural resources and industrious people, Mexico remains a poor country where most cannot afford a car and some farmers still plow with horses. The bus stops frequently, ferrying workers to and from the capital and industrial Querétaro. There, near dusk, a dark, weathered campesino perhaps in his seventies boards the bus with other seeming construction workers and, sitting next to me, eats an ear of roasted corn, turning it with paint-flecked fingers. I want to ask him how old he is and what circumstances have led him still to be laboring at his age. I know he has a story, likely tragic, as many Mexicans do. But he doesn't want to talk. Eventually the bus drops him at a hilly crossroads in the campo, and, alone, he walks off across the high desert into the rainy night.

Yes, changes — superficial and otherwise — in San Miguel. The center now gentrified with glitzy restaurants replacing the rustic, comfortable bars of years past, ostentation supplanting authenticity. On the main square the cigarette vendors and Indian women who cooked on griddles have been driven from beneath the portales by pricey cafes. The town's population has tripled, with spreading colonias now covering the surrounding hills where I used to hike in solitude. And of course technology—the cell phones, Internet cafes, cable TV, FedEx deliveries, and such—that assures one does not travel too far. Two decades earlier my general delivery letters from the States would sometimes take a month or more to arrive; packages often never came; a call home required a stroll to the *larga distancia* office where a bored teenage girl would attempt to put through the call, always an iffy proposition. Now my cell phone rings while I am sitting in a cantina, reminding me how hard it is to hide nowadays.

But in that cantina I find the Spaniard Arquimedes, who has survived the years in seeming good shape and is still full of cheer and caustic wit, of bonhomie and brotherhood. And Julio, the dentist, who tells me that Guillermo, the taxi driver whose wife, Esperanza, I helped bury, has never remarried and still drives a cab. La vida pasando, but I feel like Rip Van Winkle, as if no time has passed.

*

On my desk in Key West leans a framed print made by Arnold Schifrin to commemorate his daughter's marriage in 1986. When writing and researching this book I learned that Arnold, with whom I had lost contact during my itinerant writer's life, died in 1996. Then, in San Miguel, I learned that Lupe's husband, Gerónimo, had passed away a few years ago. Certainly others portrayed here, such as David Gray, who would be well over 100-years-old, are likely dead. Licha and Adriana are probably grandmothers. Similarly, the times depicted, though only some twenty-five years past, are dead and gone in San Miguel thanks to computers, growth and the inexorable evanescence of existence. Returning there briefly I realized how ephemeral life is, particularly its beauty. However, the raw vibrancy of my transformative years there lives on in unsullied memory, remembrances still so vivid and alive to me.

Although immersing myself in Mexico, as Schifrin had counseled, had always marked for me the beginning of a journey, I now see, after writing this memoir, that my journey had begun long before that and still continues. For a writer—or anyone striving to comprehend the world and fashion a fruitful life—there seem to be few sure answers to the enduring questions of existence and few reliable rules of conduct, except perhaps for the Mexican ones suggested to me during my early years in San Miguel de Allende: Recognize your own insignificance and that greater forces exist; understand that life is trouble and appreciate its moments of beauty; live inside your body, not just in your mind. As Ernesto warned me, "I don't like that thinking business, Rick. Gets you in trouble."

While my personal salvation came in large part through my submission to the non-rational sensual world, as a gringo who continues to live in the Anglo world, at least for the time being, I still persist in thinking too much, most likely. Perhaps it comes in part from spending too many winter days in the north—where there is no blooming bougainvillea, no scent of cilantro on the streets, no lithe Latinas entreating you to dance—and in part from isolating myself in my work. That introverted aspect of me lives on.

Nonetheless, little of my life in Mexico is lost to me. I remember all the compulsion, passion, beauty, and danger. I carry those memories with me not as rueful reminders of some paradise lost but as mandates to live fully. In them I see how hungry I was for experience, how open I was to baptism and rebirth, and how Mexico became part of me. I see how little I have changed since.

Yet now as I think back on it all, one image rises prominently, that of Adriana sitting across from me at comida in the patio of the Posada Carmina shortly after we had first met. Birdsong, warm sun, vibrant flowers, and sweet scents; her dark eyes resting on me. A moment of rare beauty, hope, and possibility. One thinks of the roads not taken, of the necessities that tear us apart, and the sweet sadness of life with all its wrong turnings and stumbling. I wonder where she is now, what road she took. And I wonder if I might not soon return to the life there that I had abandoned.

ALSO BY RICK SKWIOT

Christmas at Long Lake: A Childhood Memory

The compelling true story of a young boy's efforts, at Christmas 1953, to preserve his rural Midwest home, depicting a bygone era of uncomplaining and frugal self-reliance.

"…an elegant evocation not only of a particular time and place but also of the way childhood memories set up a permanent residence in our hearts. This is a lovely, elegiac book."
— Robert Olen Butler, Pulitzer Prize-winning author of
  A Good Scent from a Strange Mountain

Sleeping with Pancho Villa

Graceful but gritty, spare yet complex, this darkly comic yet affecting novel exposes the passions, magic, and brutality of a haunted and haunting town far south of the border. Finalist for the Willa Cather Fiction Prize.

"Life in a Mexican town…laid out beautifully…A skillfully written portrait of an entire community. Highly recommended."
— *Library Journal*

Death in Mexico

Hemingway First Novel Award winner. The passionate mystery of a son's compulsive search for his father's bones—a quest that draws him into an exotic Mexican underworld of sex, mysticism, drugs, and sudden violence.

CPSIA information can be obtained at www.ICGtesting.com
Printed in the USA
LVOW051955300613

340869LV00001B/9/P